IDRC-131e

GIVE US THE TOOLS

SCIENCE AND TECHNOLOGY FOR DEVELOPMENT

Editor: David Spurgeon

Spurgeon, D.
IDRC, Ottawa CA   IDRC-131e
    Give us the tools: science and technology for development. Ottawa,
Ont., IDRC, 1979. 190p.:ill.

    /IDRC publication/. Review of the role of /IDRC/ in fostering
/development research/ /research project/s in /developing country/s –
discusses the Centre's origins and aims; presents /case study/s of eleven
projects dealing with various aspects of development; assesses the impact of
research and its funding in developing countries.

UDC: 300.001   ISBN: 0-88936-213-0

Microfiche edition available

CONTENTS

PREFACE

TWO THEMES have been to the fore consistently throughout the international community in the past quarter-century. The first relates to political independence: the creation of autonomous national states in territories once governed from afar as part of colonial empires. The second theme is one of economic well-being: the demand of the billions of human beings living at or below the sustenance level for improved nutrition, shelter, health care and education.

Success has proved less elusive in the attainment of the first of these goals than the second. The number of independent states granted membership in the United Nations has tripled during the life of the organization, yet the standard of living of much of the world's population has risen only marginally, and this notwithstanding massive transfers of developmental assistance. A good deal of the success achieved in the political arena is now subject to tarnish if widespread economic progress cannot be achieved and sustained.

Increasingly the nations of the world are looking to science and technology to provide that progress. They do so because the application of scientific methodology and the employment of technology bear promise of success in the quest for a better life. Yet neither of these factors is self-executing. Each presumes a competence within the developing countries for wise and effective absorption of fresh knowledge and techniques.

It is to contribute to that competence as well as to support science and technology in the developmental process that the International Development Research Centre exists. This volume of essays is intended to convey to readers some description of the unique character of the Centre, its functions and its precedent-setting experiences. Fittingly, much of that description is conveyed by persons from developing countries. This is their story; it is deserving of a large and sympathetic audience.

Ivan L. Head,
President.

INTRODUCTION

I N 1969, THE PEARSON COMMISSION, a group of world leaders assembled under the auspices of the World Bank to assess the consequences of 20 years of development assistance, said in its report, *Partners in Development*: ". . . international support for development is now flagging. In some of the rich countries its feasibility, even its very purpose, is in question. The climate surrounding foreign aid programs is heavy with disillusion and distrust. . . we have reached a point of crisis. . . Our travels and studies have convinced us that we have come to a turning point. On all sides we sense a weariness and a search for new directions."

Such was the atmosphere surrounding foreign aid when the International Development Research Centre was in its formative stages. The disenchantment was due to a number of factors. Some, as the Commission pointed out, were the result of unrealistic expectations on the part of both donors and recipients. Some had to do with the inappropriate reasons aid was extended in the first place: "to achieve short-term political favours, gain strategic advantages, or promote exports from the donor." Still other reasons lay in the waste of aid funds and the growing preoccupation on the part of donors with their own domestic problems.

By the late 1960s, the world was beginning to realize that the promotion of international development was a far more complex and long-term problem than anyone had previously imagined. Simple solutions, such as the transfer of capital, which once had been believed to be the answer (as indeed capital transfers were in Europe after the second world war), were seen no longer to be sufficient.

At the same time, by the late 1960s developed-country governments were showing evidence of great expectations of science and technology. The spectacular contributions that research and development had made during the second world war, the demonstration of man's ability to explore and travel in space, and the emergence of new products and processes from the laboratories had focussed all eyes on science. Every developed country had by that time established a science policy structure, and both politician and man-on-the-street seemed convinced a future of boundless benefits awaited those countries that applied science and technology effectively to their problems.

Developing countries also were vitally interested. And the success of the Rockefeller and Ford Foundations' R&D programs with new, high-yielding varieties of rice and wheat — producing what was dubbed "the green revolution" — seemed to confirm the value of science and technology to international development.

Yet studies showed that, at that time, only about two percent of worldwide R&D was being carried out by developing countries, and that much of that was actually detrimental to their interests, involving such things as research in synthetics, which would replace their own resources or world markets. It was therefore obvious that, though science and technology promised much, this promise had not been realized for the developing part of the world.

The United Nations Organization, in fact, saw the widely growing gap in science and technology between the Third World and the industrialized countries as one of the major factors in the increasing disparity in living standards between these disparate parts of the world. In 1963 it held the United Nations Conference on the Application of Science and Technology for the Benefit of the Less Developed Areas. As a sequel to this conference, the UN set up an Advisory Committee on the Application of Science and Technology to Development. This committee noted in its third report to the UN Economic and Social Council that ". . . only a very small fraction of the world's scientific and technical resources is devoted to the problems of the developing countries; the overwhelming proportion of the world's intellectual capital, as well as its physical capital, is applied towards meeting the needs of the highly developed countries." The committee later prepared a World Plan of Action for the Application of Science and Technology to Development, listing priority areas for R&D and detailed proposals for other areas.

It was in this context that the idea for the International Development Research Centre was born. As we shall see, the IDRC was conceived as a mechanism to foster and encourage the use of science and technology for the benefit of the developing world. This book describes how the idea arose, how the early concepts were changed in the reality and what the Centre actually became.

The first two chapters are largely descriptive: they outline what happened to produce the IDRC as it is today and go on to tell how the Centre functions.

In Part Two the book presents 11 case histories of projects that illustrate different aspects of the Centre's programs, written by people in Third World countries who are familiar with them. The point of these chapters is to present an objective evaluation of representative projects by Third World experts, in order to provide readers with an independent assessment of the Centre's approach. In each case, the author was invited by the IDRC to present his views, and was provided with only general guidance as to the kind of question to be answered. The evaluations, therefore, are the authors' own.

Finally, Part Three concludes the book with an analysis in general of the role of research in solving the problems of developing countries. This chapter, written by an independent Third World scientist, assesses the impact of foreign funding agencies in general in supporting research in the Third World — and of the IDRC in particular.

As will be seen from the chapters that follow, the establishment of the IDRC constituted a novel approach to the enlistment of science and technology in the cause of development. It is only now, as the Centre approaches the end of its first decade, that an evaluation of this approach has become possible. The Centre hopes that by publishing this book it will provide a critical assessment of the approach, and by so doing contribute to the discussion that will take place at the United Nations Conference on Science and Technology in Development (UNCSTD) at Vienna in August 1979.

PART ONE

THE ORGANIZATION

CHAPTER ONE

HOW IT BEGAN

THE FIRST PUBLIC ANNOUNCEMENT of what eventually became the International Development Research Centre was made by the late Lester B. Pearson, then Prime Minister of Canada, on June 7, 1967. Speaking at a banquet of the Canadian Political Science Association at Carleton University in Ottawa (of which he later became chancellor), Mr Pearson said: "A lot of the excitement in using the new techniques for the purposes of peace and universal human progress, instead of for war and universal human destruction, is simply not getting across, either to world statesmen or to the people of the developed countries. So the Government is looking into the possibility of building on the inspiring theme of 'Man and His World' created by Expo, a Centre for International Development that might perpetuate on a more permanent basis this heightened Canadian awareness of the problems and the challenges confronting all mankind at the present time."

The timing was propitious. Celebrating their centenary that year, Canadians had felt a new sense of nationhood as visitors from all over the world flocked to the site of the international exposition, Expo 67, at Montreal. The exposition seemed to demonstrate that the "average Canadian", far from being provincial, had a vital interest in his fellowmen of all nations, and in even the most abstruse science and complex technology.

The mood of the Western world as a whole was buoyant in the '60s: it was the hey-day of space exploration, high-technology stocks were making investors a lot of money, and the oil embargoes and double-digit inflation of the '70s were not yet dreamed of. The concerns of environmentalists were heard as murmurs rather than shouts, and science and technology seemed to promise a limitless future for all.

What still remained to be done, however, was to bring the fruits of science and technology to the developing nations of the world. Somehow,

◀ *The IDRC's Board of Governors frequently holds its meetings in Third World countries — this time in Senegal.*

despite years of foreign aid programs and technical assistance, these countries, instead of gaining, were losing ground in economic and social benefits when compared with the developed world.

Said Mr Pearson to the political scientists: "The challenge for international development is to find new instruments for concentrating more attention and resources on applying the latest technology to the solution of man's economic and social problems on a global basis. One idea for a new Canadian initiative in meeting this challenge that should be considered is for the establishment of a Centre of International Development: it might even be on the site of Expo 67. After nearly 20 years of trial and error in the field of international development, we have learned a great deal about what can and cannot be done. But at the present time, there is no single institution in the world that could act as an internationally recognized focal point for concentrating attention and interest on this vital challenge to all of humanity."

Although Mr Pearson's address was the first time the idea for such a Centre had been announced publicly, discussions had been going on in Ottawa for many months. The idea originated with Maurice Strong, who at the time was the first President of the Canadian International Development Agency (CIDA).

Strong's business experience (he had once headed a large conglomerate called the Power Corporation of Canada Limited) had taught him the value of research. And he was appalled by the fact that a government agency would spend hundreds of millions of dollars on development projects without having first done any research into what kind of projects were needed.

"I came to CIDA with some rather strong views about what development assistance should be concentrating on," he recalled in 1978. "I held the very strong conviction that scientific and technological capability was one of the prime differences between developing and more-developed countries. It was this gap — in research and development and its application — that really was fundamental, because today's research produces tomorrow's technology, and tomorrow's technology is the key to tomorrow's development. As long as that gap wasn't tackled fundamentally, we were just going to be attacking the symptoms rather than root causes (of underdevelopment)."

Strong then set about determining how best the Third World's scientific and technological capabilities could be increased.

"I consulted with all kinds of people," he said. "I got a number of people within CIDA to help me consult. We looked at the Rockefeller Foundation and the Ford Foundation — we looked at a whole series of experiences, particularly in areas where there had been significant scientific and technological contributions.

"It was clear from our examination that it was going to be difficult to give to the developing countries the kind of objective assistance that would add to their own research and technological capability within the framework of a conventional development aid program. And as we didn't have private foundations of the size of the Ford and Rockefeller, we thought perhaps we should create a separate instrument."

The conviction that a new kind of agency was needed was based on a number of differences that exist between aid in science and technology areas and other forms of aid. Research takes a long time to pay off, and at best is a high-risk venture. Sometimes the payoff is difficult to discern, particularly in a quantifiable manner. So Strong thought it necessary to create an agency that was, as he puts it, "one step removed from the day-by-day political process where immediate results were going to be more accountable." In addition, Strong and his advisors believed a professional environment was necessary for such an agency, rather than the usual bureaucratic one found in government bodies.

Strong makes it clear that the IDRC developed from a need, not from anybody's desire to create a new agency. The Centre was not, in other words, a solution looking for a problem.

"In the beginning, we started with an issue: is the science and technology gap an important one? (and the answer was fairly quickly 'Yes'); if so, by what means can we best address that gap? We didn't start out saying 'We want an IDRC, what should we do?' We started out with the feeling that this gap in science and technology was a fundamental one, that not enough was being done in this area, and we asked 'How best can Canada take an important initiative in this area?' And the IDRC, after a long process, became the initiative."

Former Prime Minister of Canada, Lester B. Pearson (left), and Maurice F. Strong.

At about that time, Prime Minister Pearson and his staff were searching for a way of continuing the great public enthusiasm that had been aroused by Expo 67. One of the rules of an international exposition is that the buildings on the site must either be dismantled by the nations that built them or donated to the host country: they cannot be used again for the same purpose. Millions of dollars of imaginative real estate was thus tied up just outside of Montreal without a plan for its future. Some of the Prime Minister's advisors felt the Expo 67 site could be most usefully employed as the base for some kind of a permanent world institution.

One of the Prime Minister's staff heard of Strong's investigations into the need for new ways of supporting R&D in developing countries, and mentioned it to Pearson. So one day when Strong had joined Pearson for lunch in the Prime Minister's office, Pearson asked him about the matter.

Strong told him of his inquiries, and the result was the short mention, quoted at the beginning of this chapter, in Pearson's address to the Canadian Political Science Association. That indication of support from the Prime Minister was all that was necessary to get the momentum really going behind the idea. Strong soon afterward obtained the services of A.W.F. Plumptre, a former senior assistant deputy minister of finance, and at that time principal of Scarborough College of the University of Toronto, to undertake a study to determine if such an agency was indeed needed. He also set up an interdepartmental committee that included all the pertinent deputy ministers.

An interesting sidelight at this stage was the difficulty Strong got into with the establishment in Ottawa over his plans. After the mention of a new initiative appeared in the Prime Minister's speech, Strong received an angry phone call from Marcel Cadieux, then undersecretary of state. "I remember that conversation extremely well," says Strong. "He said, 'Maurice, let me tell you something. As a new deputy minister around here, you don't put things to ministers, and certainly not to the Prime Minister, until they've been cleared by the official structure.' He was really unhappy with me for taking this initiative. I was in trouble with the establishment. So my answer was, 'Look, the PM asked me about this. He'd heard that we were considering something like this. If the PM asked you about something like this, wouldn't you feel bound to answer? I couldn't say, 'I'm sorry, sir, I can't talk to you.'

"I did make it clear that it was still in the process of research. But I was surprised that he'd put it in his speech. I think they thought that I'd put him up to it.

"In any event, the next time I went over for lunch, I said, 'Well, Mr. Prime Minister, you got me in trouble with that thing in your speech. The whole group of officials now have got their backs up.' And Pearson said, 'Well, don't worry, Maurice, I've been around the official system a long time and I did that deliberately. You'll find it will give the idea a good boost despite what the officials say, because the Prime Minister's committed now.'

"I decided that now that the issue had surfaced — it had surfaced prematurely — the only way was to embrace the establishment and get them committed. So I went out on a search. I asked a lot of people who could I get who are so acceptable to the establishment that if, after looking at it, they give it their endorsement, the group of deputy ministers around here will have a hard time not approving it."

In a book called *Freedom and Change: Essays in Honor of Lester B. Pearson*, Wynn Plumptre said of these events:

"Paul Martin (then Minister of External Affairs) brought Strong to Ottawa in 1966 in order to give new impetus and direction to the expansion of the external aid programme. Strong's meteoric career, to the presidency of the Power Corporation of Canada Ltd. and to considerable wealth, had included associations with the United Nations in New York and with the international YMCA in Geneva. In Ottawa circles, his proposal for a research centre was considered imaginative, perhaps a bit too imaginative, and when the Cabinet considered it in July 1967, the natural decision was to set up a Steering Committee of officials to consider the scheme.

"This Committee was a formidable one. Under Strong's chairmanship it included the heads of no less than 17 departments and agencies including, of course, such obvious ones as the Privy Council; External Affairs; Finance; Treasury Board; Industry, Trade and Commerce; Agriculture; Energy, Mines and Resources; and the Science Secretariat."

At the time all this was going on, there were widely divergent ideas among the proponents about what kind of agency the proposed centre should be. Strong had suggested research on such world issues as urbanization, the resources of the sea, climate control and educational television. He was quoted in the press as seeing the Centre as "the natural home for the creative eccentric." He said "some of the great minds of our times are going to be attracted here by this." Plumptre writes that Strong thought of people like Barbara Ward, Kenneth Galbraith and Marshal McLuhan as primary actors on the centre stage.

Pearson was also attracted by the "think-tank" concept. Plumptre says that the possibility of launching the centre on a multinational basis had occurred to Pearson as early as 1967, and he had even wondered if it could not become a specialized agency of the United Nations Organization. Even after the Centre was formed and began to take other, more practical directions, Pearson continued to think in these terms, Plumptre says: "His interest was much easier to arouse in a think-tank type of project, for example in an appraisal from a developing-country viewpoint of the sombre World Model articulated by the Club of Rome, than in the general run of grassroot projects sponsored by the Centre."

The newspapers and magazines of the day reflect these early conceptions. Peter Newman, then a syndicated columnist, now editor of

Maclean's magazine, spoke of it as "a sort of world-wide university on a grandiose scale. . . an academic institution comparable in stature to the Brookings Institute (sic) in Washington," where "some of the world's leading intellectuals (would) direct themselves to the solution of mankind's pressing problems." *Time* magazine claimed it would be "a think factory, on the order of California's Rand Corporation."

Some in Ottawa were also considering an additional function for the centre, besides the problems of the developing world: that of domestic policy analysis. Pearson stepped down as Prime Minister before plans for the centre came to fruition, and the new Trudeau government wanted a centre set up that would look at domestic policy questions. For a time, both domestic and international questions were considered as possible functions because many domestic issues had their counterparts on the international scene. Eventually, however, the domestic policy analysis function was handed over to another new institute set up in Montreal for that purpose: the Institute for Research on Public Policy, whose Ottawa office, by coincidence, now resides in the same building as IDRC.

Another early preoccupation was with information. Some, including Pearson, saw the proposed centre as a repository of vast amounts of information — a kind of enormous data bank — that developing countries could draw on for research.

Not all those involved in the early planning agreed with all these ideas. There were questions about whether a new aid agency was needed at all, in view of all the other agencies existing — and if it was, whether the best place to put it was Canada. There were questions about the proposed site, about the kinds of people proposed by Maurice Strong to carry out the work of the centre, and the kinds of project proposed. Some asked whether, if the idea were to create a think-tank, the funds ought not to go straight to Canadian universities.

To answer such questions, and to determine whether there really was a need for a new development agency in view of the many already in existence, Plumptre visited 24 agencies abroad. These included government departments in Washington, Paris and London, United Nations development agencies, the World Bank, the Commonwealth Secretariat and leading universities and foundations. The results of the inquiry were positive. Says Plumptre:

"The Report disclosed, first and foremost, complete unanimity in favour of the proposal that the Canadian government should establish a development research centre. There was an urgent international need for additional research of the type envisaged. Moreover, Canada, which had access to advanced modern technology yet was not tainted by colonialism, was exceptionally well-placed to provide it. Reference was also made to the fact that Canada would communicate in either French or English."

While Plumptre found unanimous agreement that a centre was needed, he also found unanimous opposition to the idea that it should take the form of a think-tank. Great stress was laid on the need for the research to be done in the developing countries, and that the research should be action-oriented, practical research designed to solve specific Third World problems, rather than basic research.

"There were universal indications, amongst the various institutions and agencies that were visited," says Plumptre, "of a willingness to cooperate and collaborate with the proposed Canadian centre. A welcome was forthcoming for the suggestion that some linkage might be created between the new centre and other bodies involved in development research by the appointment of persons connected with the latter to the governing body or to advisory committees of the former.

"On the other hand, when the question was raised whether the Canadian government ought to think of seeking the cooperation of other governments in the establishment of a full-fledged international organization, the reaction recorded in the Report was strongly negative. An intergovernmental body would take years to organize, would be cumbersome to operate, and could not be endowed with the special advantages that seemed to attach to a research centre that was launched and supported by the Canadian government and was rooted in Canadian experience and expertise."

In the evolution of the Centre, two factors most influenced the course of its development: this report by Wynn Plumptre and its subsequent endorsation by the Steering Committee and the Cabinet; and the arrival on the scene of David Hopper, who was chosen to be the Centre's first President and chief executive.

One of the contributions of Plumptre's report was to introduce the concept of mutual benefit to Canada and Third World nations. The Centre's basic objective, he said, "should be to develop research that responded to the needs of developing countries and which at the same time had application to Canadian experience and Canadian problems."

The Steering Committee then prepared its own report. That report proposed an independent, non-profit organization sponsored by Canada that would both do research itself and contract research out to institutions in Canada and the developing countries. This report had the Centre defining developing country priorities for research and co-ordinating research in Canada and abroad. The data-banking role was emphasized, Plumptre's report notwithstanding, as was the domestic role of research with Canadian implications. The paper was submitted to Cabinet on September 3, 1968, not much more than a year after Pearson's first announcement of the government's intention to set up a Centre, but by now Pierre Trudeau was Prime Minister. The Throne Speech later that month indicated the new government's intention to proceed with legislation establishing the Centre.

When the legislation creating the Centre was finally drafted (by James Pfeifer, now Secretary of the IDRC), it established, as Lester Pearson (then the Centre's first Chairman) said at the first Board of Governors' meeting in October, 1970, "something that is unique in international organizations." It was a public corporation, to be financed by appropriations made annually by the Canadian Parliament (with provision for funds from other agencies if that were to be considered desirable), but with its direction and control through a board of 21 members, of whom 10 were non-Canadians. Said Pearson: "I know of no other institution that has been constituted in this unique and very encouraging way." (In practice, a number of the 10 non-Canadian members of the Board of Governors have always come from developing countries: on the first board there were six. The President of the Centre is always a member.)

The corporation was not to be part of the public service, was to be tax-exempt, and was not to be subject to the usual Treasury Board rules for Crown corporations or to certain sections of the financial administration that would have hampered the role seen for it. It was also "not an agent of Her Majesty."

In *The Evolution of the International Development Research Centre, An Interpretation,* * Shirley Seward, now a program officer in the Centre's Population Dynamics and Policies Program, says:

"The acceptance of such a corporation by the Department of Justice and the Treasury Board was the result of the influence of Maurice Strong, and a work of legal art on the part of Pfeifer. Moreover, it should be recognized that such acceptance was a reflection also of the favourable, though not indiscriminate, disposition of several officials and ministers."

The purpose of the Centre, as defined in the Act (which was given Royal Assent May 13, 1970) was "to initiate, encourage, support and conduct research into the problems of the developing regions of the world and into the means for applying and adapting scientific, technical and other knowledge to the economic and social advancement of those regions." In carrying out these objects, the Centre was "to enlist the talents of natural and social scientists and technologists of Canada and other countries; to assist the developing regions to build up the research capabilities, the innovative skills and the institutions required to solve their problems; to encourage generally the coordination of international development research; and to foster cooperation in research on development problems between the developed and developing regions for their mutual benefit."

The Act thus made it possible for the Centre to fund research either in developing countries or in Canada, carried out either by developing country researchers or Canadians. It also made it possible for the Centre "to establish, maintain and operate information and data centres and facilities for research and other activities relevant to its objects." It was, in fact, an extremely broad and flexible piece of legislation.

*Internal IDRC document. This paper contains extensive historical information that was freely drawn upon for this chapter.

The direction that the Centre actually took in interpreting how this legislation should be enacted was a result, first, of concepts put forth by Mitchell Sharp, the Minister for External Affairs, in his speech in the Commons during second reading of the bill, and later of the leadership of David Hopper as first President. Sharp, in a speech drafted by Maurice Strong, said the Centre: "Will give high priority to programs that assist the developing countries to build their own scientific and technological capabilities so that they will not be mere welfare recipients, but contributors in their own right to the solution of their own problems."

The strongest influence on the shaping of the Centre, however, was David Hopper. "Once David came," says Maurice Strong, "it became his Centre."

David Hopper was admirably equipped, by education, training, experience, temperament and outlook to transform the Centre from a paper creation to a reality. A native of Ottawa, he acquired a BSc degree in agriculture at McGill University, spent two years in India doing research, then took a PhD at Cornell University in agricultural economics and cultural anthropology. After spending several years teaching at the Ontario Agricultural College, Ohio State University and the University of Chicago, he returned to India as an agricultural economist with the Ford Foundation, and became involved with work that led to the green revolution. At the same time, he was a consultant to the World Bank, and immediately before coming to the Centre was associate field director of the Indian Agricultural Program with the Rockefeller Foundation.

Hopper's experience in India, which included some time living in a village and experiencing rural peoples' concerns first-hand, gave him a keen understanding of Third World problems. He had seen the fallacy of trying to transfer directly the experience and methods of North American farming to Third World conditions. And he had developed a healthy respect for the abilities and resourcefulness of the Indian farmer. But his work with the new, high-yielding varieties of wheat and the techniques of the green revolution with the Ford and Rockefeller programs had convinced him that science had much to give to rural people.

"In the perspective of man's evolution," said Hopper, "social and material progress has arisen from only two sources: altered technical relationships among the factors used in the process of production, and the enhancement of human skills and abilities."

He saw the Centre as an instrument "for the modernization of traditional or ancient peoples," and he was convinced that what he called "the eventual metamorphosis from neolithic to modern" was inevitable for all mankind. "To suggest that modern technology or the means to its development should be shunned because it appears to carry with its adoption uncertain and unwanted side effects begs the crucial issues of our times," he said. "The alternative to scientifically derived technology is not a society free of the effects of technology, it is a stagnant society. . . . All human culture rests on some form of technology, and within the short span of a few generations it will be founded universally on the rationality of applied science."

To Hopper, the abundance that scientific technology brings promised the elimination of human want. "It is this that fascinates the world's poor." But frustrated rage might replace the fascination if the promise were not realized by more than a few people. And "too often in the two-decade history of international development the share of the poor in progress is reckoned zero." Progress now would have to be measured in terms of satisfying real human need, "not as an end product of an heroic accounting exercise."

It was therefore important, Hopper told the first Governors' meeting, that great care be exercised in choosing the focus of the Centre's efforts. "We seek to apply science directly and through research to the needs of development, and to help in creating in developing regions a capacity that will enable them to bring to bear the methods of scientific enquiry to the solution of their own problems," he said.

Hopper saw the Centre as a public corporation whose directors were the Governors; "our shareholders, the people of Canada; our clients, the world's poor." But the clientele should be more closely defined: the Centre's program, he suggested, should aim to promote "the welfare of peoples, both farm and non-farm, living in rural areas throughout the world." His concern was chiefly for the rural poor, he said, because they were most directly affected by the process of modernization occurring throughout the Third World, and the Centre's program should "seek to find ways to bring help to those who are least able to benefit immediately from presently available technologies."

Hopper recognized that by so sharpening the focus he was excluding large areas in need of research. But it was his deliberate choice to sharply delineate the boundaries of Centre interest until its resources and management capacity were adequate to larger programs.

Nor did sharpening the focus mean making it narrow: "Indeed, the whole space of rural life would hold our attention: education, local government and administration, social institutions, the measures necessary to protect and preserve the rural environment, and the physical health of the rural family are but a few of the issues encompassed by the umbrella."

Hopper then outlined what he called "the style of the Centre's operation." It would not have a large in-house research capacity, he said. Contracts and short-term consultancies or staff appointments would provide flexibility for the management and prevent a surfeit of obsolete talent.

Wherever possible the Centre's aim would be to involve several institutions and countries in its grants. And "to allay the charge that we are dictating priorities, I propose that we use our resources to supplement locally supported activities" and that local research workers' opportunities should be expanded to allow collaboration with those engaged in similar problems elsewhere in the world. Travel funds would be provided for researchers from one Third World country to visit those from another — something then difficult to find. "Because of the nature of most aid arrangements," said Hopper, "it has been easier to bring an African or an Asian research worker to North America or Europe, or to send a North American or European to Africa or Asia, than to effect visits by Africans and Asians across their national and regional borders."

Hopper proposed that the major portion of the Centre's funds should go to institutions and professionals in low-income countries. And he saw as the most significant of the corporate objectives the one that charged it with assisting developing regions of the world to build up their research capabilities, innovative skills, and institutions to solve their own problems.

The Centre's staff, Hopper said, would have a high level of professional competence and skill, and a respect for the personal and cultural heritage of their colleagues in developing countries. The bulk of the Centre's funds would be concentrated on problems of regional and international significance, not just those of interest to one country. And a substantial allocation of its funds would be used for training of personnel, usually as a component of a specific project.

One of the most important of Hopper's proposals, and one that turned out (as we shall see from later chapters) to most impress developing country people with the Centre's sincerity, was then outlined by Hopper in these words: "In establishing the Centre's stance toward co-operating institutions and research workers, I hold that it must be founded on a confidence that they, not we, are the best judges of what is relevant to their circumstances. Until this confidence is proven misplaced, I will be content to leave the direct management of our support in the hands of our partners, reserving to ourselves only the rights of audit and periodic substantive review." If a particular project involved the collaboration of several parties, Hopper said they would be encouraged to devise their own techniques for self-monitoring, "so that a minimum of overall supervision will be required from us."

And then, in what turned out to be a prophetic statement, Hopper told that first Board meeting: "If this is successful, we will have pioneered a new style of international operation that can remove the stigma of charity and donor control from the support of research in development."

Almost two-and-a-half years after he outlined his guidelines for Centre operations at the first Board of Governors' meeting, Hopper reflected on what had been accomplished and what lay ahead. Looking toward a new phase of Centre development, which would be marked by the appointment of six new governors, Hopper posed 11 policy issues that had arisen during the experience of those first 30 months. (*Research Policy: Eleven Issues*, W. David Hopper, IDRC-014e)

Referring first to the objectives set out in the IDRC Act, Hopper noted that the Centre had so far emphasized the recruitment of scientific and technical staff from Canada and abroad, and the enhancement of the research skills of their counterparts in the developing countries. Particular emphasis had fallen on the latter.

These two goals, he noted, had been more vigorously pursued than the other two: "to encourage generally the coordination of international development research; and to foster cooperation in research on development problems between the developed and developing regions for their mutual benefit."

"I hope," said Hopper, "to be able to report to subsequent Board meetings substantially greater progress in attaining these objectives."

Hopper then went on to deal with the 11 policy issues. He first stated the issue, then outlined Centre policy in that area, and finally described the Centre's experience in previous months. Included in the latter part were some recommendations for future policy.

The issues he listed included the following: striking a balance between Centre support for Third World researchers and for developed country researchers; between Centre support for projects designed primarily by Third World people and those reflecting Centre priorities; between projects that would give experience to Third World researchers and those that would produce the highest quality research results. Others included were the balance between problem-oriented and basic research; between institution building, research training and research support; between support for speci-

The IDRC's first President, W. David Hopper (left) and his successor, Ivan L. Head.

fic projects and for general assistance to institutions; between support for research and for post-secondary or post-graduate training; between support for specific projects and non-specific grants to research associations and networks; between support for analytical research and for action projects; between support for research on uniquely national problems and for global or multi-nation problems. Finally, he questioned the Centre's predominant focus on rural people.

Although some shift in emphasis was apparent in this presentation, it is remarkable how little the basic policy of the Centre was changed by it. Important as it was in providing an opportunity for the Board of Governors to pause and reconsider Centre policy, Hopper's paper basically amounted to a refinement of his original policy guidelines — guidelines that have defined Centre policy until this day.

David Hopper left the Centre near the end of 1977 to take up new duties as Vice-President for South Asia at the World Bank in Washington. Before he left a search committee of the Board of Governors was set up under the chairmanship of Maurice Strong to look for a successor. After some months of study and deliberation, the committee made its recommendation to the Board of Governors, the Board in turn made its recommendation to the Cabinet (as stipulated in the IDRC Act), and in March, 1978, Ivan L. Head was appointed President.

A native of Calgary and graduate of the University of Alberta in arts and law, Head received his LL.M. degree from Harvard University in 1960, where he was a Frank Knox Memorial Fellow. Following his admission to the bar, Head practiced law in Calgary for several years and later joined Canada's department of External Affairs. As a foreign service officer, Head served first in Ottawa and later in Southeast Asia. In 1963 he was back at the University of Alberta, this time not as a student but as a professor, and in 1967-68 he left again to serve as Associate Counsel, Constitution, to the Minister of Justice of Canada.

That Minister of Justice was Pierre Elliott Trudeau, and when Trudeau became Prime Minister in 1968, Head joined his office as Special Assistant. For the greater part of the next 10 years, Head's special responsibility was foreign policy and the conduct of international relations — a preparation that served admirably as an introduction to his role at the IDRC. During this period, Head advised the Prime Minister on his Commonwealth and foreign activities, acted as the Prime Minister's special representative on missions abroad, and served on Canadian delegations to a large number of international conferences.

His experience naturally leads him to view the Centre in terms of a broad fabric of international activities. "In 1979," he said recently, "there is not only UNCSTD in Vienna, but also UNCTAD V to be held in Manila (the fifth United Nations Conference on Trade and Development); the Commonwealth Heads of Government Conference in Lusaka; and the Multinational

Trade Negotiations in Geneva. And we are in an advanced stage of preparations for the special session of the United Nations General Assembly next year on the subject of development. The IDRC must be seen to operate in this context."

Head feels the IDRC has now matured to a point where it must have more formal planning and evaluation mechanisms, and these have in fact been introduced since his appointment in March, 1978. He also believes it should be looking to possible involvement in new areas of research, such as renewable energy for developing countries. Some moves have already begun in this direction, for example with studies on the utilization of biomass and wind energy.

Head has continually voiced his adherence to the original broad concepts of Centre policy, such as the need to continue to follow the priorities of developing countries in research, and the independence of the Centre from the Canadian government. His view of the Centre's role was perhaps best expressed in an address he gave to a conference on world food security at York University in Toronto in March, 1979:

"Evidence now reveals clearly that development is a beneficial operation in which all win, or in default of which all lose. . . One can treat the New International Economic Order as an emotive slogan, as many have done, and derive considerable mileage from it. Conversely, one can employ the phrase as a rallying cry around which people of goodwill congregate in order to pursue the task of building a better world for all of us. In this latter sense, this constructive sense, there is a need to solve problems, to build up skills and competence that by themselves may appear minute but in the aggregate are critical. There fits the role of the IDRC: one that is benign yet all the while crucial."

CHAPTER TWO

HOW IT WORKS

A VISITOR TO MALAYSIA flying into Kuala Lumpur will see spread
out on the rolling hills below, acre upon acre of small trees with
dark green fronds set out neatly in rows. They are plantations of oil
palms, which are gradually replacing the rubber plantations of former times.
In recent years the oil palm has become Malaysia's second most important
crop, the product of its fruits being much in demand for the production of
margarine and other edible oil products.

But the mills that extract the oil have recently become an environmental menace: most of the river basins, particularly along the west coast of
the country, are being polluted by wastes from these plants. And the rivers
are the chief source of drinking water.

The mills spew out not only suspended and dissolved waste material, which depletes the water's oxygen, leaving it foul and malodorous, but
also phenols, which produce a particular stench of their own and prevent
people from using the water. Unfortunately there is often no other unpol-
luted source of water for the inhabitants of small villages downstream. Few
plants control their waste discharges, and the problem has reached serious
proportions. Most of the mills, being owned by smallholders or cooperatives, cannot afford the existing waste water treatment technology.

In 1977, Malaysia's Department of the Environment (DOE) commissioned a short-term study of the problem by the Asian Institute of Technology (AIT) in Thailand, with the help of funds from the United Nations
Development Programme. But a more detailed study, involving research
with waste treatment technologies, was needed before DOE could draw up
enforceable regulations against discharge of untreated water. The AIT made
a proposal to the Malaysians for such a study, but DOE did not have the
funds to carry it out.

In September 1977, DOE wrote to the director of the IDRC's Asia
Regional Office in Singapore to ask if funds would be available for such a

project. What followed culminated in a grant of $84,600 to AIT and the DOE in January, 1978. The way in which this came about helps to explain how the IDRC operates.

The Centre has four program divisions: Agriculture, Food and Nutrition Sciences; Health Sciences; Information Sciences; and Social Sciences. Each of these divisions has a number of operational programs which are the responsibility of professional staff, most of whom have long experience in the Third World, and travel widely in search of projects the Centre can fund. Most have a network of contacts from previous sojourns overseas.

The Centre also operates regional offices in Singapore (Asia), Dakar (Africa), Cairo (Middle East), and Bogota (Latin America and the Caribbean). A fifth regional office in Nairobi was recently closed due to budgetary restrictions that have affected all Canadian government-financed agencies. It is hoped that the closure will be temporary. These offices are also staffed by professionals who represent the four program divisions, and who keep the head office staff closely in touch with local conditions.

When the director of the Asian Regional Office, Jingjai Hanchanlash, received the request from DOE, he first studied it with the help of his professional staff, then replied to DOE, telling them that Michael McGarry, Associate Director in charge of the Rural Water Supply and Sanitation program of the Health Sciences Division, would be passing through the region on October 31. McGarry was well-known to Malaysian environment ministry personnel from the days when he had been a professor of environmental engineering at AIT. A meeting was arranged for that day between McGarry, two of ASRO's staff, and DOE, to discuss the proposal.

Between that first meeting and the following May, when AIT first presented a formal proposal to the Centre for funds, a great deal of activity took place on both sides. The IDRC staff studied the scientific literature on the subject to determine what work had already been done in Malaysia, and whether other countries might better be suited to carry out such a project because of their experience with the problem. For its part, DOE surveyed Malaysia's technical resources to carry out the project, finally deciding that AIT personnel in Thailand were best equipped. The process was prolonged when a Malaysian, who was first identified to direct the Malaysian component of the project, was killed in an automobile accident.

A Malaysian commercial laboratory also was identified to do waste water analyses, provide technical assistance and run laboratory scale waste treatment units. The final project thus became a joint endeavour of the Asian Institute of Technology in Thailand and the Department of the Environment in Malaysia.

Once McGarry had received the proposal from AIT, he was able to start the procedures going in the Centre that would produce the grant. On May 1 he prepared what is known internally as a Project Notification Memorandum. This is simply an initiating document setting out the broad objec-

Malaysian farmer harvesting oil palm kernels.

tives of the proposed project and the approximate level of funding required.

The Projects Committee is a committee of the Centre established to advise the President: it meets prior to meetings of the Executive Committee and the Board of Governors, and is composed of the President (who is Chairman), the Senior Vice-President, the Vice-President Planning, the Vice-President Administration, the Secretary, the Treasurer, all Program Directors, and representatives from the following government departments: the Canadian International Development Agency, the Treasury Board, the Department of External Affairs, the Ministry of State for Science and Technology, and the Department of Industry, Trade and Commerce.

If the PNM receives a favourable response from the Projects Committee, it may be placed on the agenda of a future meeting for consideration as a more fully-developed project, or it may be placed on the agenda of the next meeting of the Centre's Governors.

In the case of "Palm Oil Wastes (Malaysia)", as the project now became known on Centre documents, the Projects Committee recommended approval in principle at its meeting of May 12, 1978. The PNM then was placed on the agenda of the June 10, 1978, Board of Governors meeting (held in Ottawa), and there too it received approval in principle.

Following this a Project Summary was prepared by the Health Sciences Division. This document is a much more comprehensive one than the PNM, including details about the background, objectives, methodology, administration, and budget. This summary went by mail to each of the Governors on December 1, 1978, together with a memo on background information. The Governors have 30 days to communicate their observations or objections. If no objections are received the project is deemed approved.

In this case, the Board members approved the project, and on January 2 an authorization was drawn up for the signature of the President to say that the grant could be released. On January 31 the Centre received a cable from its regional office saying the grant letter had been signed by AIT officials and giving the information on the bank to which the money should be paid.

Thus 16 months after the first contact was made with the IDRC, the project funds were in hand. This case is not entirely typical (few are!) because approximately six months were lost as a result of the death of one of those involved in the project. It also involved three separate visits from IDRC personnel — one from Ottawa — and two visits by the AIT leader. But it serves as an example of how the Centre operates.

The cornerstone of the IDRC's policy is its insistence that the research projects it funds should be identified, designed, conducted and managed by developing country researchers in their own countries, in terms of their own priorities. But there are other criteria as well. To be approved, a project should have a useful application over a region, not just in the country in which the research takes place. It must in almost all cases be practical research, oriented toward the solution of a problem, rather than simply adding to existing knowledge. It must help improve the living standards of those countries it is designed to help, and lessen the gap in development between rural and urban areas. It must make the fullest possible use of local resources and research workers from the region. It should result in better-trained and more experienced researchers, and more effective research institutions. In most cases there must be a local contribution of funds to the project, or at least a contribution of time and facilities. And it must fall within the areas of concentration chosen by the Centre.

These areas of concentration are fairly broad, as the following descriptions of the Centre's four program divisions show:

AGRICULTURE, FOOD AND NUTRITION SCIENCES

Highest priority in this Division has been assigned to the food and tree crops of the arid and semi-arid tropics; to root crops, which provide basic subsistence for more than 300 million people; to artisanal fisheries and small-scale fish culture; to by-products and agricultural wastes as animal feed on small farms; and to combined farming systems that will most benefit the poorer rural communities.

About 50 percent of the Division's budget has supported crops and cropping systems research; 21 percent animal sciences research; 11 percent fisheries and forestry research; and seven percent research on post-production systems (processing, storage, food preservation, distribution and use in the home).

The main object of the Division's projects is to improve the health and economic well-being of the rural poor. Thus crops such as sorghum, millets, food legumes, oilseeds and root crops are emphasized. The animal science program has recently been expanded to integrate livestock management, improved pasturelands, and research on feed supplements from by-products and wastes.

In fisheries, much attention is being given to aquaculture, and improved methods of preservation and processing of fish. In forestry, emphasis is on savanna cultivation and the use of trees to protect crops, conserve land and provide fuel for the rural people of the semi-arid tropics.

In post-production systems, emphasis is on rural grain, legume and oilseed processing and other farm storage systems, while a new emphasis has been added to the application of wind and solar energy to food processing. There is support for projects oriented to the rural consumer, and a number of projects are soon to be launched, in collaboration with the Health Sciences Division, to improve the nutritional well-being of the people who live in the drought-ridden areas of the Sahel and in semi-arid tropical areas.

HEALTH SCIENCES

From the inception of its program until 1975, the Health Sciences Division included demography and family planning studies, and was known as the Population and Health Sciences Division. In that year, demography studies were shifted to the Social Sciences Division and family planning action research was de-emphasized because of the large amount of resources being directed into that field by other international agencies. The Health Sciences Division program is now conducted in four areas: fertility regulation methods; tropical diseases; rural health care; and rural water supply and sanitation.

In fertility regulation, the emphasis has been on the support of international, regional and national activities, the international focus being the International Committee on Contraceptive Research. The committee's aim is the development of new contraceptive methods and improvement of currently-used ones. Attempts are made to gain greater acceptance of these methods and also to minimize health hazards.

The Division also provides research grants to promising Third World scientists to continue work in the field of human reproduction in their own countries.

Tropical disease research is supported partly through the WHO Special Programme for Research and Training in Tropical Diseases and partly through outside studies on gastroenteritis, with special reference to viral causes; the possible effects of excessive cassava consumption in areas with limited iodine uptake; and dengue hemorrhagic fever, which has become prominent in Southeast Asia and has spread into most Pacific islands.

The rural health care studies are designed to provide minimum services through the use of various types of health care worker, from village volunteers and traditional workers to low-level auxiliary personnel. Manpower studies are also carried out.

During recent years activities in water supply and sanitation have included studies of latrines and compost toilets, handpumps, windmills and the reclamation and re-use of animal and human wastes. Links are also made with large donor agencies so that the results of research can be fed into their projects.

INFORMATION SCIENCES

Although the original concept of the Centre as a vast information bank did not materialize, the importance of information was embodied in the Act and the Centre is one of the few aid agencies to have a program devoted to information problems. The Information Sciences Division program encourages the sharing of information resources. Many of its projects have consequently been developed within the framework of the international cooperative bibliographic information systems organized by UN agencies. These systems are intended to remedy the defects, from the developing countries' point of view, of the information services of the industrialized world — high cost, need for foreign exchange, reliance on well-developed library networks, and, most important, poor coverage of the developing countries' own literature. By inputting their own literature to these systems, participating countries in return have access to the literature of the rest of the world. Many IS grants are helping developing countries participate through regional centres for agricultural, population and socio-economic information, which act as a link to the international systems and provide output services specially tailored to local needs. In the field of economic and social information, the Centre has, in addition, taken the initiative in promoting an international system to serve development planners and policymakers. Attention is also now being paid to developing national information infrastructures to enable countries to organize their own information more effectively.

In Ottawa, the division operates a developmental library, open to the Canadian development community and to developing-country users. For library management purposes, information retrieval from the library's holdings and for special bibliographies, a computer system, called MINISIS, has been developed to run on a minicomputer cheap enough to be dedicated to bibliographic work. MINISIS incorporates many of the features of ISIS, a bibliographic system for big computers used by many international agencies and initially for the Centre's library. Centre staff have directly assisted developing-country institutions to implement ISIS. Arrangements are now being made to transfer MINISIS also, for local services and for participation in international systems.

From the outset considerable importance has been given to specialized information centres dealing with very specific topics, such as particular tropical crops. Typically, these centres collect relevant literature identified by means of the big systems, abstract it, analyze data, publish special bibliographies and newsletters, commission reviews, answer questions and provide documents. Like the Cassava Information Center described in Chapter 13, they are located at centres of excellence where scientists and information specialists can work side by side.

As well as supporting information systems that handle large numbers of documents, IS projects meet the needs of particular clienteles in other ways. Two of these — a magazine on family health and development for francophone Africa, and a network of institutions training extension engineers to take problem-solving information to small industry — are described in Chapters 7 and 12. The production of maps for development purposes, particularly by using data collected by satellites, is also of importance, and there is a small research program into mass communications techniques applied to rural development.

SOCIAL SCIENCES

The Social Sciences Division's program has been oriented toward an understanding of the processes of development, modernization and change in the Third World. Studies seek to understand how and why change occurs, and its effects on people, government and institutions. The purpose is not simply understanding for its own sake, but understanding in order to better effectuate the kinds of changes Third World leaders desire for their people.

One element, for example, is the science and technology policy program described in Chapters 4 and 5. Research in this area is designed to assist policymakers to understand societal implications of technological choices, and to help them design policies dealing with technology and science that will produce the desired improvements in their societies.

Rural modernization efforts continue to be a major concern in virtually every developing country, and the socio-economic aspects of these are a focus for Centre projects. Another focus is the management of development activities: in the past, donor countries assumed that all that was necessary for efficient administration of development activities was to transfer Western management methods and solutions, just as economists and bankers had argued that the vital factor in development was capital. Experience has shown both ideas to be wrong, and research is now necessary to find appropriate alternatives.

The population dynamics and policies program has two objectives: increasing scientific understanding of how social and economic patterns in

developing countries are influenced by population growth, structure and distribution, and what the relative advantages are of the different policy options in these areas. But while most support has been for studies evaluating
population policy and program alternatives, two other major areas of interest have been research on the determinants of fertility and on the impact of
population distribution policies.

The focus of the education program is on the primary school system: how best to provide universal primary education in a Third World setting, and assessment of the experiences of children once they leave primary
school. The problem to be overcome is how to raise the quality and extend
the coverage of primary schools without raising costs.

These highlights of the Division's programs can only convey at best
a sketchy picture of the Centre's activities, but they do give some idea of
their scope. In general, the Centre has attempted to fund areas that have
been neglected by other agencies, and those that seem most likely to have a
direct effect on the Centre's chief clients, the rural poor.

The geographical distribution of the Centre's projects can be seen in
the accompanying table. For 1977-78, Parliament's annual grant was for
$34.5 million.

PROGRAM PROJECTS
APPROVED TO 31 MARCH 1978
($1000's)

Region of Activity	PROGRAM DIVISIONS							
	Agricul-ture, Food & Nutrition Sciences	Informa-tion Sciences	Health Sciences	Social Sciences & Human Resources	Publica-tions	Canada & Donor Agency Relations	TOTAL	% of TOTAL
Africa	13 979	2 817	3 814	2 667	—	491	23 768	18.76
Asia	16 190	4 247	6 272	11 672	132	74	38 532	30.42
Middle East	5 877	962	587	358	—	160	7 944	6.27
Caribbean and Latin America	10 554	3 199	4 779	7 878	39	—	26 449	20.88
Global	2 098	1 485	3 254	5 742	—	655	13 234	10.45
Canada	2 378	2 359	424	11 241	7	294	16 703	13.18
TOTAL	51 076	15 069	19 130	39 558	178	1 674	126 685	
% OF TOTAL	40.32	11.89	15.10	31.23	0.14	1.32		100%

Since the Centre became operational in October, 1970, it had, by
March 31, 1978, approved 690 projects requiring appropriations of $120 mil-
lion. These projects lasted from as little as six months to three or four years.
Some idea of the size and proportion of the activities of the various divisions
can be gained from the number of projects undertaken and the amount they
cost during 1977-78: Agriculture, Food and Nutrition Sciences, 63 new pro-

jects, $10.6 million; Health Sciences, 41 projects, $3.5 million; Information Sciences, 25 projects, $3.4 million; and Social Sciences, 50 projects, $9 million.

There is a special budget of about $1.8 million for the Human Resources Awards program, which allows professionals from Canada and the developing countries to undertake research and training in the various fields of international development. Awards in this program are available in a number of categories.

The Centre also supports a number of international agencies and has been at least partly responsible for the establishment of several new ones. In the human resources field, the Centre contributes to the Southeast Asia Population Research Awards Program, supported jointly with the Ford Foundation; the Agricultural Development Council's training program in Asia; the Council for Asian Manpower Studies; and the Social Science Research Training Program of the University of Indonesia.

The Centre is a member of the Consultative Group on International Agricultural Research (CGIAR), which supports a network of international research centres devoted to increasing food production in developing countries. And it has played a part in setting up three new institutes in this network: the Institute for Crops Research in the Semi-Arid Tropics (ICRISAT); the International Livestock Centre for Africa (ILCA); and the International Centre for Agricultural Research in Dry Areas (ICARDA). It has also established the new International Council for Research on Agroforestry (ICRAF).

The Centre's relationship to CIDA is fraternal but independent. Unlike CIDA, the Centre "is not an agency of Her Majesty," as the IDRC Act put it. However, the Centre has kept close ties with that agency and in fact has acted as manager for a number of research projects on its behalf. The most significant current one is a project in Kenya in the control of wildlife diseases.

In simple terms CIDA's work involves capital-intensive projects for development, contributions to multilateral agencies such as the World Bank, food transfers, and technical training programs. The IDRC's involves research for development, and a Canadian component is neither necessary nor often desirable, since the object is to build up the research capacity of developing countries.

The chapters that follow describe a number of Centre projects in some detail, and evaluate their effects on the countries involved in them. The examples have been selected from all four program divisions, but they are not in any real sense "typical" projects. In fact it would be extremely difficult to select *any* project as being typical of the Centre's work, such is the variety involved.

It is hoped these case histories will provide a useful assessment of the outcome of the IDRC experiment by independent developing country observers.

PART TWO

THE PROJECTS

CHAPTER THREE

SCIENCE, TECHNOLOGY AND SOCIETY

JORGE A. SABATO

How can science and technology best be employed to serve the interests of developing countries? In an attempt to find answers to this question, the IDRC has supported more than 50 developing country teams in 35 countries to carry out research in science and technology policies. This research has been wide-ranging, including global studies on a computer modelling of the world situation; regional technology policy studies, as with the Andean Pact and the Caribbean; national studies of science and technology policy implementation, as with the Science and Technology Policy Instruments (STPI) projects; micro-level studies such as the management of technology and the absorption and diffusion of imported technology in Asia; and studies on the social and economic effects of specific technologies, such as biogas and gari. The Centre has also joined with the United Nations University in supporting the study of how to link the R&D systems in a developing country with the problems of rural areas. Approximately one-third of the research in this program has been concerned with broad national and regional policy issues, another third with technology policies and decisions made by industrial enterprises, and the remaining third with the linkage between the two.

◄ *Bringing research to the people — an extension worker talks with farmers.*

 To obtain a Third World overview of this program, the IDRC interviewed JORGE SABATO, research professor and member of the Board of Directors of the Fundación Bariloche, Argentina. A former physicist, metallurgist and director of the Technology Branch of the Argentine Atomic Energy Commission, Dr Sabato now does research in science, technology and development. A former senior research associate with the IDRC, he has published half-a-dozen books and more than 100 papers.

I DRC — Dr Sabato, what would you say were the main strengths and weaknesses of the Centre's science and technology policy program? And is it possible to make any assessment of the impact of this program on the development of the Third World?

Sabato — I would like to be very emphatic in saying that as far as I know this science and technology policy program has been by far the most successful one ever carried out by any international organization. This is not only my personal opinion — it is what I have heard all over the world when I speak to colleagues in other Third World countries.

I think that I can substantiate this. The first point is what I would call the substance of the IDRC program. When this program was inaugurated seven years ago, many Third World countries were already involved in science and technology activities, but the theoretical knowledge for those activities was rather weak. The conventional wisdom of the time was that every country must have a scientific infrastructure (a national research council, laboratories, research centres and training institutions), and once you have it, technology will automatically flow from good science. This was the Vannevar Bush approach of the '40s in the United States, when he wrote a famous letter to Franklin Roosevelt proposing a science program for the United States. Bush's ideas were widely accepted and the gospel was propagated everywhere.

By the end of the '60s there were some in the Third World who began to suspect that the conventional wisdom was not enough, that the theory was a bit superficial, and that in fact if a scientific and technical infrastructure is a *necessary* condition for every country, it is still not a *sufficient* one. So it was the right time for the IDRC to come in with a program that was going to delve into the relationship between science and technology and society — not only the relationship between technology and economic

growth; or science, technology and development; but the relationship between science, technology and society. The question to be considered was, in
which ways can science and technology be applied for the best development
of a country? The moment was ripe, and in fact people in the Third World
were beginning to discuss a new orientation for science and technology policy, but to find that orientation it was obviously necessary to have a better
theoretical background.

So policy research was a critical necessity at that time: without it,
we would be operating in the dark as we had been before. Just copying the
philosophy or the theory behind the development of science and technology
in developed countries was a trap. It was because they just copied what the
Americans did, or the Russians did, without a deep analysis of the cultural,
historical, social and economic circumstances surrounding the problem, that
some of the efforts carried out in the '50s and the early '60s did not lead anywhere, except to train more people. The IDRC program arrived just in time!

The second issue behind the success of the science and technology
policy program, I think, was its approach — an approach, incidentally, that
captured the philosophy of the Centre as a whole. First, the full responsibility for research would be in the hands of Third World people, from its choice
and definition, through its execution, to its completion. No other international organization before that was courageous enough to trust the capabilities, the intelligence, the honesty of Third World researchers and say,
well you have the ball, you go and play, without being "controlled" by big
brother. This was a key issue. The program trusted the quality of people in
the Third World and it also gave them the opportunity to develop their own
capabilities.

Another important component was the idea of having more than
one country involved in a network — an idea that led to the cooperation of
researchers from different Third World countries. A lot of people were saying that cooperation was the fundamental thing. But cooperation is a cultural
process, it works through individuals. You must develop linkages between
people. When the program was established, those involved in science policy
research in the Third World were quite isolated. They were just beginning to
make some connections through meetings, and as a result they discovered
that they had much more in common than they imagined — but they still
didn't have the chance to get together and work together. When the program
established the principle of a network of institutions, it was doing something
very important — it was creating an "invisible college" of Third World scholars. This was a really fundamental point, because once the program is over
you can be sure that the invisible college will remain.

Another important point about the Centre's program is the way it
was organized, and the relationship between the Third World researchers
and the program headquarters. One key to its success was the idea of manag-
ing this program from a university (Sussex), rather than from a building full

of bureaucrats. This was quite an innovation at the time — and still is. For us, it was important that we had the chance to discuss things in a place full of ideas and committed to the same kind of issues we were discussing.

IDRC — Why has the program been considered a success?

Sabato — Thanks to the program, we know better what to do. We now have a real arsenal of knowledge. We know more, and more in depth and over a broader spectrum, and in many aspects that were ignored completely seven or ten years ago. So much so that we from the Third World can now go to any meeting with our colleagues from the developed world, and not be second-best any more. We are considered intellectual equals. This is why I say the world of science and technology policy is quite different for us today than it was seven years ago. People in the Third World now are writing papers and books on science and technology issues that are considered excellent material by our colleagues in the developed world. And a very interesting thing has happened: because this confidence has developed, we now look at our counterparts there more as colleagues than as enemies or big brothers.

IDRC — One of the projects supported by the program was concerned with the Andean Pact. This project attempted to develop regional technology policies. It also developed specific action plans for the technological development of industrial sectors. The political problems of the Pact appear to have led to a lessening of commitment on the part of governments to the general policies, such as Decision 24 on foreign investments. But the detailed sectoral plans are still being implemented. I wonder what you infer from this? Is there much point in carrying out general policy research? What was the impact of the IDRC support to the Andean Pact and would the Andean Pact studies have been done anyway without IDRC help?

Sabato — The Andean Pact program has at least two dimensions that are important. One we can call the academic dimension, the other the political dimension. It also has a demonstration effect that I will analyze later.

Let's begin with the academic dimension. It is important to remember that the Andean Pact was trying to propose a piece of legislation on foreign investment, linking capital and technology explicitly. Until then, in every piece of legislation of each of the six countries involved, only the capital side of foreign investment was contemplated explicitly. Technology was there only as a ghost — it never was put in explicitly. And the political and economic consequences of that were very important. But in order to pass a new piece of legislation involving both, it was necessary to do research, to understand more, to go deeper into an understanding of the relationship between foreign investment and technology. And this is exactly what the program did.

The main academic consequence was that the nature of technology as a commodity was clarified. Up to that project, technology was seen more as applied science, as diffusion of techniques, training of people, diffusion of handbooks or written material. Technology was analyzed more in the abstract, not in a very concrete economic dimension. What the project did was give the opportunity to really go into depth in the analysis of technology in the productive structure, and the nature of technology as a commodity became clear. This concept is perhaps one of the richest in science and technology policy or science and technology in development — and not only for the Third World countries. Before the project, other people had said that technology could be analyzed as a commodity. But the Centre project put a lot of emphasis on it, and used it as one of its key concepts.

Another important concept — the consequence of the first — is that instead of talking about the *transfer* of technology, as was common at the time, it was recognized that it was better to talk about the *commerce* of technology. This difference may not seem very important today, but at the time it was quite something. We discovered in this project that in fact the majority of the technology that circulates in the productive structure is not by any means free. You pay for it. So if you pay for it (and you have to pay very heavily at times) transfer is a misleading term, and so instead of talking about "donors" and "recipients" we must talk about "sellers" and "buyers".

Now when you talk about sellers and buyers, many things immediately become clear: the semantic curtain that was hiding important economic and political phenomena behind the so-called transfer of technology opens up. It is important to analyze the seller-buyer contract in technology commerce, and particularly to read the fine print of contracts. Believe it or not, until about ten years ago, the fine print of technology contracts was never analyzed clearly in the open, or at least in the literature. The consequence was that a lot of unfair practices were in common use — some that the code of conduct of the transfer of technology now being discussed at UNCTAD, is trying to deal with. In a sense UNCTAD's code of conduct is a direct consequence of some of the studies performed under the project.

Now I would like to deal with the demonstration effect of the second part of the project. Once Decision 24 was passed, two other decisions were passed specifically on technology policies: Decisions 84 and 85. One deals with patents, trademarks and all industrial property rights in the region. The other one defined a common regional technology policy, one of the elements of this technology policy being the *Projectos Andinos de Desarrollo Technologico*. The purpose is not just to do studies on technology, but to perform scientific and technological activities in common. For example there is one program on copper, another on forestry, etc. The program on copper involves Bolivia, Peru and Chile: there is a common program for the three countries using laboratories, personnel and material resources from each to carry out for some years a very well-defined and specific technological program. The main purpose is the developing of new ways of processing copper.

There is a demonstration effect because they try not only to get a new technological process but also to prove that it is possible to have researchers and institutions of different countries working together in a common program, with a very concrete target.

IDRC — Would the Andean Pact studies have been done anyway with or without IDRC help?

Sabato — That is difficult to answer. The Andean Pact was a very young institution when this study began. The governments did not have any experience in this kind of game. The Andean Pact members were very conscious that it was necessary to carry out research into technology and foreign investments. If not, they would not be able to draft the legislation they were supposed to draft. So my feeling is that the IDRC assistance was strategically essential: it appeared at the right moment and gave, so to speak, the flexibility and the support they needed.

IDRC — Another project supported by the IDRC program was the Science and Technology Policy Instruments (STPI) project. It linked countries from Asia, the Middle East and Latin America together in a network to study ways and means of implementing technology policy. One of the principal conclusions was that the explicit policies for technology formulated by science and technology councils had relatively little impact on the technology decisions of people working in industrial enterprises. They appeared to be much more influenced by other government policies in the economic and fiscal areas. What do you think are the implications of this finding for technology policy in developing countries?

Sabato — The STPI project is one of the most interesting ever carried out, because for the first time a team of researchers from ten different countries on three continents tried to carry out a critical analysis of what was done in science and technology policy in those countries during the last 15-20 years.

Before I answer your question I would like to indicate some of the characteristics of the STPI project that made it interesting. The first is that it was the most ambitious network ever built for a project, a network of countries of completely different histories, traditions, and economic development. Another valuable aspect is that STPI contains a critical review of actions taken by various countries. They are not just theories or ideas, but concrete actions — what happened with national research councils and registries of technology in different countries, and so on. This provides policy-makers, particularly in less developed countries, with a kind of guide — if you like a kind of "Guide Michelin" of science and technology instruments, with the results of these actions. It is a critical review that tries to determine whether the actions were successful or not, and why.

STPI, in my opinion, was a very good approach. It was not just a strict analysis of every piece of legislation — that would not only be very boring, but I would not consider it very educational either. The way the team approached the issue was not only to analyze every action but also to look into the background. For example, one of the studies — one of the best I ever came across — is on the influence of state-owned enterprises on technology policies. The approach had enough generality to allow us to distinguish some of the theoretical mistakes in some of the policy instruments. And the preoccupation was always to know what was behind every instrument.

I am not surprised that one of the findings of the studies was — as you have mentioned — that technology policy has been quite divorced from technology practice. This is a clear demonstration that technology policy cannot be defined by the science policy of the country. For the conventional wisdom of the '50s, technology is just applied science, and so if we have the right science policy we're going to have the right technology policy. This is a fallacy. In a sense it was the most deplorable myth of the '50s and '60s. Now it has been proved, and it is no longer just an opinion, that the practice of technology policy has been different from the rhetoric, because practice links technology policy to economic policy more than to science policy.

A technology policy must be part and parcel of economic policy, for the simple reason that technology is a social event that happens in the productive structure of the society. You don't have technology in a vacuum. Technology is always mixed up with the productive structure, and so technology policy cannot be separated from economic policy. STPI has made a major contribution in proving empirically that this is the case.

IDRC — You are familiar of course with the Bariloche Foundation world model. When the Centre agreed to help fund this project, some members of the press in Canada were critical, on the ground that this was a very academic study of limited value to development. However, the Centre's publication on this project *Catastrophe or New Society?* (IDRC-064e) has turned out to be a best seller. Why do you think there has been so much demand and do you agree with critics who say that the study was too academic? What has the response to the study been among Latin American governments and particularly the response of the Argentinian government?

Sabato — I suppose the demand for the publication is high because people are very interested. Now why are they interested? Before the Bariloche study was funded, the Club of Rome's study *Limits to Growth* was published and produced a lot of noise all over the world. When we studied that report at the Bariloche Foundation, our reaction was that this was a typical study made from the North by the North and with the hypotheses of the North. The study had the prestige of the people who did it, the institution where the study was performed (MIT) and also the fact that it used computers — computer models always impress the layman. When we had read the study, we said: If we ask the same questions from the South — from the underdeveloped world — what kind of answer are we going to get?

The answers are very different from those of *Limits of Growth*. This does not mean that our study is better or more correct than theirs, it's just a different study. One interesting result of our study is that there are *no* physical limits to growth in general terms. The real limits to growth are socio-political limits. So if we don't make transformations in the socio-political aspects of society, there are going to be important problems in the future. I imagine that it has produced a lot of interest, particularly in the Third World, to have a Third World analysis of the future of the world. I suppose this explains the popular success of the book. Also the academic criticism has been quite generous to us, in the sense that the reviews have been very good. It has not been heavily attacked — I don't remember any attacks saying that the study has made technical mistakes. Of course the approach is different from others, and you can agree or not with the hypothesis and also with the target. We define very precisely what the purpose of the exercise was: to try to determine if there were any limits to maintaining a population of about fifteen thousand million inhabitants in the world in the year 2025 and supplying their basic needs. Our main hypothesis was that every human being, by the mere fact of being born, has the right to satisfy his basic needs.

IDRC — So you do not agree with the critics who say that the project was too academic?

Sabato — No. Completely the other way around. The objective of the project was not academic but political, exactly as in the case of *Limits to Growth*. And in both projects, carried out academically, the consequences are political. For example, if you take the case of Latin America and you analyze the possibility of sustaining the population of, say, two thousand million inhabitants in the next twenty years — and providing the basic needs of all this population — the answer of our model is that there is no physical limitation. There is only one limitation — land ownership. If the land remains a private asset then there is no solution. But if you transform land into a free good, the study shows Latin America in 20 years' time can satisfy the needs of all its inhabitants. If this is not a practical result, I don't know what is.

　　　　You asked about government reactions. The reaction of Latin American governments in general has not been very favourable. One reason is that governments or politicians are not much interested in what is going to happen in 20, 40 or 50 years' time. This is not so only in Latin America — you have had your own experience in Canada. Governments are worried about short-term problems. Secondly, the hypotheses or the predictions of the model were not very palatable to some governments for very obvious reasons. Anyway, I don't think this is peculiar to Latin America. Governments have not been impressed by other models either. The Club of Rome — and I belong to the club — has been knocking on the doors of governments for the last ten years, trying to call attention to what the club calls global problems. The answer has been practically nil, except rhetorically. But I am sure that these types of ideas are going to influence future policies.

IDRC — The Centre's science and technology policy program in general has tried to be responsive to the research needs and problems identified by researchers in the developing world. One result has been a heavy emphasis on science and technology policy studies concerned with industrialization, with little support for studies on agriculture and other aspects of development. Only recently there appears to be emerging an interest in the developing world, for example, in technology policy studies related to rural development. How do you explain this imbalance? You could argue that the IDRC itself should have recognized the imbalance of its programs several years ago, and rectified the situation. But I wonder what your response is to the suggestion that the Centre should determine priority for research in science and technology policy?

Sabato — Yes, there was a stronger bias toward industrialization than toward agriculture. The main reason was that every country was trying to become industrialized, following the conventional wisdom of the '60s and '70s, and so industry was growing anyway. Every country was then becoming industrialized and so the imbalance of the program was a product of the time — it couldn't be otherwise. Now, why didn't the IDRC itself have the imagination to push more research on rural development? In my opinion, it was not a question of imagination but of being consistent with the IDRC approach, which says to developing countries: "You choose, and if you make a mistake it will be your own mistake." This, I think, is a very proper attitude. I like to be responsible for my own mistakes. I don't like to pay for the mistakes of others. I am quite happy that IDRC didn't try to dictate the norms and the procedures to be followed. The Centre should *not* determine priorities for the Third World!

IDRC — There have been very few requests for support of projects concerned with science policy studies as distinct from technology policy studies. Why do you think this is the case? What sort of science policy projects would you like to see the Centre support?

Sabato — I think that again this corresponds to what was happening in our countries. It was the spirit of the time: "Let's forget about science for the time being and let's try to understand what technology is." Now, I think, we are in a better position to ask questions about science, not only science as related to technology, but science as related to society. We need now to do in science what we did in technology, to have a fresh approach, to understand that many of the answers that have been proposed have been very superficial — not only in less-developed countries but also in well-developed countries. We need to dig deeper into the relationship between science and society, and so I would endorse studies of an interdisciplinary nature on the relationship between science and other aspects of society — for example, science and philosophy, science and history, anthropology, political development, and the arts, and last but not least, science and technology.

IDRC — If the Centre continues to follow the policy of only supporting work of developing country researchers and excludes researchers in the

North, might it not fail to come to grips with some of the critical North-South technology policy issues? What in your view are the most important of these issues that deserve further research?

Sabato — If we are able to define North-South problems, I would suggest having mixed research teams from the North and the South working together on an equal basis, and led by the most capable of those involved. The policy

Cable factory in Peru — what choice of technology?

followed by IDRC up to now has been the correct one: let the people in the South deal with their own problems. But if we are talking about North-South problems, I think it would be better to have the perspectives of both involved. It is very clear that we have areas of cooperation and areas of conflict. For example, there are global problems such as earthquake or weather control, or the use of river and ocean basins. In these problems cooperation is convenient, necessary and possible. But the areas where technology is a commodity are areas of conflict and negotiation, and not areas of cooperation. It is better to get rid of the hypocrisy that we are all brothers and that we are always going to cooperate in all areas. It is not true and it cannot be true!

IDRC — There is a trade-off in all the Centre's programs between providing support to researchers with an international reputation who produce the highest quality research, and taking risks helping new, often young researchers to get started. The science and technology program is trying to keep approximately a 50/50 balance between the "generation of knowledge" objectives and the "training of new researchers" objectives. However, when money gets tight, there is a tendency to take the safe option. How important do you consider it to be to encourage research even when the results are likely to make only a little addition to the body of the world knowledge?

Sabato — Absolutely fundamental. Try to keep 50/50 as a minimum in the sense of promoting new people. In fact one of the important aspects of this program is that a lot of new people have been discovered and promoted. And they have produced some of the best results. I think it may be necessary to sacrifice quality in the short-term in the interests of future potential for the Third World.

IDRC — The science and technology policy program as a whole has supported a wide variety of studies. Do you think it is appropriate that it should continue to support this wide spectrum of topics, or do you think it would have been better to concentrate on one or two? And how important is it that the Centre should keep its professional approach, with the staff being professionals in their own activities?

Sabato — One of the really wise things the program did was to operate over a broad spectrum. And for one simple reason: we were exploring. We did not know what were the real key issues. Nobody could play God in the choice of studies, and I distrust bureaucrats who suppose that they can tell beforehand what is relevant or irrelevant. This gave us the opportunity to dig deeply into the issues, and for the first time have a view of the complexity of the problem.

Regarding Centre staff, I think one of the best elements of this program for us in the Third World has been that we were always dealing with professionally capable people. One intelligent aspect of the program, I think, was the review process: how Geoff Oldham managed to control us without giving us the impression that he was doing so — controlling in the good sense of the word. He did a very simple thing. He asked that a progress report be presented not to an office, but to a panel of people of high calibre from both the developed and the less-developed world. From the point of view of the IDRC, you get to know exactly what is going on. From the point of view of the person presenting the report, he gets feedback from his colleagues that is useful because they are intelligent people. They are not going to say, "Well, we don't like it very much, it's better that you do such and such. . ." They will say, "Why haven't you studied this, you know there is a new paper published by so and so. . . there is some research going on in some place, and I recommend this book, and so on." As you were judged by your peers, you respected their judgment. And you naturally followed their advice. Moreover, you respected the way the program was directed.

IDRC — I wonder if we can look at the future a bit, and if you can tell us what innovations you would like to see the Centre adopt in this area of research?

Sabato — Before thinking of innovations, I would recommend very strongly that the Centre not introduce changes just for the sake of changes. Secondly, beware of introducing bureaucratic elements just because you like to have a "better control", and because you would like to have the paperwork more streamlined. Beware of changing philosophy and attitude just because you would like to have a more centralized, or more Canadian approach. One of the best things about these programs is that the Canadians have not been in the foreground but in the background. The direct consequence of that is tremendous goodwill for the Canadians.

The innovations would be only perhaps in two directions. One is to promote some more complex type of study on the issue of science and technology in society, for example historical and philosophical analysis. The historical aspects of many of the science and technology analyses have been very very superficial and we need to dig deeper. The philosophy of technology is a quite underdeveloped subject everywhere and deserves much more attention.

In the organization, I am not able to propose anything very new. One suggestion however would be for an opportunity for the senior people in science policy in several developing countries to be able to come together to discuss certain issues in depth. Out of this would come an exchange of experience and also in all probability a clearer definition of research priorities. But these are not really novel ideas. So I will say finally keep going, please don't change for the sake of change, and particularly don't go in the wrong direction. Prestige that took years to be won could disappear very quickly!

CHAPTER FOUR

MAKING INDUSTRY COMPETITIVE

KUN MO CHUNG

Science and technology are key elements in improving the production capacities and competitiveness of an industrial economy. But policy instruments are required to relate science and technology to the development objectives of developing countries. In order to identify appropriate instruments for LDCs, the IDRC has funded a multi-country series of studies under the title Science and Technology Policy Instruments (STPI). The first grant, for $485,472, was made in 1972; the second, for $450,962, in 1973; and the third, for $163,205, also in 1973. This chapter describes the origins, modus operandi and some of the findings of the STPI project.

 KUN MO CHUNG, a nuclear engineer, is the former coordinator of the STPI project in Korea. A nuclear engineer, he received his graduate education in both public administration and applied physics. The Korea Advanced Institute of Science, a graduate school of applied science and engineering, was based on Dr Chung's original proposal. He currently heads the international program in nuclear engineering at the Polytechnic Institute of New York.

CONVINCED THAT SCIENCE AND TECHNOLOGY must play an important role in the industrialization process, a group of scientists, engineers, economists and policy analysts from ten developing nations conducted a cooperative, comparative policy research project — the Science and Technology Policy Instruments (STPI) Project. The project was to seek the appropriate science and technology policies consistent with industrial development strategies, and to find effective instruments to implement these policies.

The STPI project, however, turned out to be a unique experiment. It was a project designed and performed by Third World researchers, who gained invaluable experience for themselves in working with other Third World counterparts. It involved a wide spectrum of specialists, many of whom rarely had opportunities for professional interaction with experts in other areas. It was not research in the pure sense: the exchange of experience was more important than finding new knowledge. It was oriented for action: action in government and action in industry. More important was that the researchers gained new perspectives on the problems of developing countries. Close examination of such issues as technological self-reliance, technological diplomacy, consulting engineers and design organizations, and evaluation of industrial technology, gave the participants a long-term, broad view of the technological system in the context of economic development.

The participating nations were Argentina, Brazil, Colombia, Egypt, India, Korea (South), Mexico, Peru, Venezuela, and Yugoslavia (Macedonia). Although their socio-political and cultural background varied widely, substantial agreement could be drawn from the research findings. Also, through the project, it became clear that technology policy must be integrated closely with economic policy in order to be practical and to become implemented. Finally, the STPI project proved that "action-oriented" policy research can be carried out in less-developed countries.

BACKGROUND AND FORMATION OF THE PROJECT

When the idea of the STPI project was initially discussed informally among participants at a meeting of Latin American science policy organizations in Cuzco, Peru, most of the science policy research in developing countries had been carried out in Latin America and India. The awareness that technology is a key element in the competitiveness of an industrial economy and in improving productivity led to widespread enthusiasm in promoting science and technology in developing countries. However, it soon became clear that promotion of science, alone, would not provide the needed technological inputs, and that the intricacies of the mechanisms of technological activity in the economy were not adequately understood, especially in developing countries.

Early research in Latin America and India identified more problems than solutions. Convinced of the need for a more thorough study, the International Development Research Centre initiated the STPI project with full consideration of the unique environment of the developing countries. The careful attention given to this environment in the first days of project formulation was a remarkable step — a step that basically characterized the STPI project.

When the participants in the project formulation workshop at Barbados returned to their home countries and conveyed its outline to potential participants, they found an enthusiastic response. The unusual message from the Barbados meeting contained the following information:

— Although the STPI project would be funded by IDRC, an aid organization of a developed country, the project would be entirely in the hands of researchers from developing countries. There would not be any strings attached to the research grant. It was evident that IDRC was not trying to "teach" developing countries. There was no mention of experts from developed countries who would undertake major project roles.

— The selection of participating countries was not limited by political and economical considerations. There was a communist country as well as a strong anti-communist country. A number of countries were resource-rich but a few were not.

— The research was going to be "action-oriented". To many scientists, engineers and policymakers, "action-oriented" meant that the research would be useful in real life and would provide an opportunity to test policy ideas in a systematic way.

— The project was not limited to specialists in policy studies. In fact, participation of non-specialists was highly encouraged.

— There would be continuous interaction among researchers in participating countries through informal workshops and coordinating meetings.

— The research would require extensive field visits to industrial firms to obtain raw data and conduct case studies.

Because the objectives of the individual country studies and the methodological guidelines were not firmed-up at the Barbados meeting and were intentionally left to the research participants, the country teams were able to define the individual STPI projects with a clear mandate. During the initial months, all kinds of ideas and propositions arose about what to do and how to do it. (In retrospect, to many participants this initial period was the most exciting and also the most educational).

After heated discussion and numerous amendments, the methodological guidelines were accepted at the second coordinators' meeting in Mexico City. (Theoretically, the coordinators' meeting was in charge of the STPI project. Coordinators of the participating research teams formed the ad hoc council and directed the field coordinator). The adaptation of the methodological guidelines of the project itself was a major achievement, since it contains the theoretical framework for the research. This framework would become the basis of the STPI model for technology policy in industrialization.

During the early phase of the STPI project, everyone realized that there already existed a large volume of literature on S&T policies, and that policy analysts in Latin America were well ahead of anybody else in the field. It was also realized that this rich body of policy studies had not helped Latin American countries to forge ahead in technological development. In fact, the rapid growth of S&T activities in Asian countries drew envious attention from other participants. Naturally, Asian researchers became interested in Latin American policy studies and vice versa. To this complementary pairing, other participating nations added broadened references to test policy ideas and findings. The resulting international collaborative spirit was a natural happening and became a strong motive force among the entire STPI network throughout the project's duration.

AN ACTION-ORIENTED PROJECT

One of the central ideas of the STPI project was to conduct research that would have a direct impact on science and technology policy formulation and implementation in government and industry. The term "action-oriented research" was used to describe this characteristic: to provide positive advice to decision-makers, based on solid, respectable work — data gathering, analysis and problem solving.

Although the idea of action-oriented research immediately drew acceptance from the participating teams, it became clear that its implementation would be difficult. Generation of policy alternatives is the easier part; incorporating new policy ideas into the political-economic system requires thorough understanding of that system. The decision-making hierarchy is a dynamic system and involves many actors. Under the rapidly changing conditions in the developing countries, coordination among different agencies requires authoritative power and persistent persuasion.

The STPI research teams were stationed either at government agencies or educational institutions. Two countries had teams in governmental planning agencies. These teams were intimately related to economic planning and had solid foundations into which research findings from the project could be incorporated. The action-oriented research was an extension of the normal duties of the research teams.

Four national teams operated the STPI project at the government agencies in charge of science and technology. They were involved in forum formulating and executing science policies in their countries. Most of these teams, however, soon found that they must learn about *technology* policy rather than *science* policy.

Science policies are to generate basic scientific knowledge and to develop a base of scientific activities; technology policies are to acquire technical capabilities for the production of goods and the provision of services. Thus science policies are geared to support basic and applied research that generate basic knowledge, whereas technology policies foster adaptation and design activities that generate ready-to-use knowledge for localized industries and users.

Policy instruments can be classified into "explicit", "implicit" and "contextual". "Explicit" policies are designed explicitly for the policy goals set in connection with the science and technology system. "Implicit" policies are those exerting influences on the S&T system even though they were designed for other purposes. "Contextual" factors are actually political-social-cultural constraints that cannot be changed easily. Explicit science policies and their instruments were often found to be ineffective in promoting or influencing technological activities in industry.

These teams, which have considerable experience in science policy, conducted vigorous research work in technology policy. The STPI project became a strong instrument for reorienting the traditional science policy into a balanced science-and-technology policy by elevating the elements of technical policy. One team based its work at a regional social science research institute and later moved to an industrial research institute. For the team, the action-oriented aspect of the STPI project was of second priority due to the changing political situation in the country.

Similarly, two of the three teams based at academic institutions carried out research-oriented STPI projects. Instead of being involved in the decision-making processes, these teams concentrated on the data-gathering and analyses of the S&T policies.

One team, which was also based at an academic institution, approached the STPI project in a unique way. Recognizing the difficulty of carrying out action-oriented research at an academic institution, it consciously devised several features in its STPI project. They are:

1. The team invited a number of governmental and industrial planners and decision-makers to be the team's advisors and critics. Not only officials in science and technology proper, but also other officials who handle implicit policies were invited to join and help the team.

2. Team members involved themselves in industrial activities that heavily involve high-technology, as advisors and consultants.

3. Team members served on various governmental committees and rendered their services in drafting and reviewing policy papers.

4. Team members acted as liaison between the existing volumes of policy research papers overseas and the policymakers in the country. Also, the STPI team functioned as a sounding board for pending actions by decision-makers. Through free discussions, the team members provided critical comments on the ideas presented by the decision-makers.

5. During the entire course of the project the STPI team never promoted single pre-judged policy alternatives to the policymakers. Rather it would formulate a number of policy alternatives and discuss their merits and shortcomings. The choice among alternatives was entirely left to the decision-makers.

As the STPI team and decision-makers gained confidence in each other, the STPI team succeeded in making major inputs into the policy-making process. Although the team never sought any recognition for their contribution, its members are still in government and industry.

The action-oriented aspect of policy research requires a sacrifice. Since most real-life problems are complicated by a large number of factors, one usually cannot simplify them enough to make possible a thorough policy analysis. Yet these problems require action, and action must be taken in time. Very often policy making must proceed with only limited knowledge and "bad" solutions are adopted in favour of "worse" solutions. Decision-making under imperfect conditions and adoption of less-than-satisfactory solutions calls for actions that many policy analysts would have tried to avoid in the first place. If a research project sets out to be action-oriented, the project becomes a "learning" project rather than a "teaching" project. Since researchers wish to find new knowledge that can be transmitted to others, the STPI research team had to give up the teaching and credit-taking aspect of research work. This is not acceptable to many serious policy analysts, but it does not bother engineers and scientists whose ambitions are less likely to be in the area of policy research. In this sense, the early decision to invite non-policy analysts to the STPI project turned out to be a smart move in many participating countries.

It is difficult and unwise to recognize individual contributions by the STPI project teams in actual policy-making. Such recognition should be given to the decision-makers in government and industry. However, there have been many instances of positive contributions by the STPI teams. The teams were instrumental in introducing new R&D funding formats; evaluation techniques for investment projects; import regulations for foreign technologies; the use of state enterprises to increase adaptation of foreign technologies; reorganization of research institutions; the use of promotional measures for consulting engineers and design organizations; the introduction of technology policy into economic planning; tax incentives for technological activities; standardization and quality control, etc. Although the formal project ceased to function two years ago, the activities of STPI members are still continuing in all project countries.

TECHNOLOGICAL DEVELOPMENT IN LDCs

The pattern of technological development is strongly influenced by the industrialization process in LDCs. Detailed analysis of the relationship between the science and technology system and industry in STPI countries has shown time and again that local science and technology development is entirely dependent upon the level and content of industry. In other words, the real and long-lasting impact of the indigenous science and technology system is controlled by the demand for science and technology generated by industry. (This observation is consistent with the finding that implicit policy instruments are much more important than explicit policy instruments).

This research finding was accepted readily by economists and social scientists of the STPI network, but it was a startling conclusion to scientists and engineers who had dedicated themselves to promoting S&T, building S&T infrastructures, increasing R&D funding and direct state intervention in the technological activities of industries. Regardless of the socio-political background and economic characteristics of the participating STPI countries, it soon became clear that there were common industrialization and technological development features among them. In none of these countries was modern industry developed gradually, based mainly on local indigenous innovations.

Invariably, modern industries in the STPI countries owed much to the abrupt introduction of technology and facilities from abroad. Transfer of foreign technology (and investment of foreign capital) is a critical factor in developing local technological systems and industrial activities in LDCs. Therefore, industrial growth and technological development in LDCs is dependent upon the openness of the governments in the international market. (Mao's policy in China was often used in STPI meetings as a clear example contradicting the usual pattern of technological development and industrialization found in LDCs. Recent events involving normalizing of relations between the United States and China indicate strongly that even China cannot be cited as an exceptional case.)

The poor capital market in LDCs necessitates strong intervention by the government in obtaining capital for industrialization. In some STPI countries, the needed capital was furnished by the primary sector, mainly agriculture. However, the free-market mechanism was too slow in generating the needed capital. One STPI country hastened its industrialization by borrowing foreign capital and linking its industry directly to the international market. The strategy was bold in the sense that the policymakers overcame their inherent dislike and fear of foreign capital, which was closely linked in their minds to colonialism. Every one of the STPI countries was either a colony at one time, or a virtual economic colony at another time. Psychologically and politically, trying to attract foreign capital is still politically risky in many LDCs. (This situation has been much relieved in recent years with the emergence of various international funds and the huge flow of capital into OPEC countries, mostly LDCs).

Reliance on foreign capital and the increasing importance of overseas markets have exerted a strong influence on domestic technological development. Invariably, imported foreign capital means some imported technology, and the tolerance of the competitive international market for inferior technology is very small. Protectionism for infant domestic industries could be justified in many STPI countries, but it takes time to remove protective measures to improve efficiency and stimulate viable growth. In fact, the STPI studies showed that protected industrialization was harmful in developing local technological capability.

The creation of a local science and technology infrastructure is a necessary condition for indigenous technological development, but is by no means a sufficient condition. In fact, one of the major STPI themes (and findings) is that the most important science and technology policy is the "creation of demand" for science and technology in industry. Furthermore, the STPI study shows that forced demand by direct state intervention may be feasible but is rarely desirable. In rapid industrialization, science and technology considerations are secondary to economic considerations. Even enlightened planners with long-term views are reluctant to accept explicit policy instruments that would help promote local science and technology at the expense of quality and reliability. The key, again, is in finding implicit policies that create sustained demand for science and technology.

In order to identify such policies and policy instruments, one must ascertain the characteristics of industrialization and technology development. Among STPI countries, industrialization can be classified basically into two patterns: import substitution industrialization (in a pure form in Latin American countries and a modified form in others) and export promotion industrialization. Korea represents the clear-cut case of the latter.

In the import substitution model, the motive force is twofold: (1) unfavorable deficits in the trade and payments balance encourage domestic products and reduce imports, and (2) shortage of products on the international market forces domestic production. In many countries following the import substitution model, local funding was available for the initial investment. Gradually local industry shifted its emphasis from light to basic and capital goods industry. In the early stages, the role of the primary sector is essential, providing food and raw materials, foreign exchange, and low-cost labour. The import substitution model was well suited to Latin American countries, which accumulated substantial foreign exchange and experienced commodity shortages during WWII. However, after the boom of raw materials exports, these countries experienced serious constraints in industrialization. The transition to capital goods industry required concentration of capital and protectionism, which slowed down the development of domestic consumer markets and indigenous technological development. The recent reorientation of these import-substitution economies includes the promotion of exports, the inducement of foreign investments and the enhancement of technology transfer. These features are in fact the basic properties of the export-promotion model.

The widely accepted understanding of how industry technology develops is described by the "normal" flow or evolution. Production technology is evolved from a basic scientific discovery in the research laboratory. Through development research, engineering study, design and production effort, the new scientific discovery is transformed into products. Marketing activities disseminate the products and the public starts to enjoy the fruits of scientific, technological and productive endeavours. However, the introduction of new products and the associated industrial activities in LDCs rarely follow the normal flow. Invariably, importation of foreign products creates a domestic market suddenly or creates awareness of an existing market overseas.

Once the market is formed, production starts with imported parts and technology. Specifications for the product or the device are dictated by the buyers. In order to meet the specifications, foreign designs and/or foreign engineering services are purchased. In the early stages, manufacturers and decision-makers are chiefly concerned with adequate operation of turnkey plants and trouble-shooting. Only after stabilization of the initial production are attempts made to unpackage the designs. *Reverse engineering* is the natural consequence of this effort. As manufacturing experience is accumulated and the market pressure for efficiency and new designs are mounted, serious attempts are made to redesign the products. As the reverse flow indicates, further advances in industrialization proceed with domestic engineering studies and optimization processes.

Since most scientific and technical communities in LDCs try to follow the normal flow, whereas industry follows the reverse flow, integration of the S&T community and industry is feasible when the reverse flow of industrial technology meets the normal flow of S&T activities. Thus, technology policy in LDCs must promote the rapid expansion of reverse engi-

Many of Korea's industries are highly sophisticated — like the plywood company and electronics factory above.

neering activities and direct the existing S&T activities to match with the industrial activities. This attitude — and formulation of the appropriate technology policy — are easy to articulate, but difficult to implement. An entirely new view must be fully accepted by policymakers in government and industry, scientists and engineers.

EMERGENCE OF TECHNO-ECONOMIC VIEW

The strong influence of an industrialization strategy on the science and technology system through control of "demand" for science and technology was clearly and repeatedly shown in the analyses carried out by the STPI network. Sectoral priorities, industrial financing schemes, price controls, etc. in concert with industrialization determine the level, quality and contents of scientific and technological activities. Thus the question of how to formulate a technology policy consistent with the goals of economic development becomes one of how to integrate potentially divergent views between development economists and scientists and engineers. These divergent views may result in opposing recommendations.

Scientists, whose main interests lie in promoting science for science's sake, resist any state intervention in setting the direction and the control of research. They argue that the general growth of science eventually helps technological development and therefore the state should provide ample, unrestricted financial assistance to scientific activities. Detailed programming of scientific activities should be left to individual scientists, they argue. The most state intervention scientists tolerate is a broad outline of objectives and orientation expressed in a high-level policy statement.

This view is strong among basic scientists who have only remote contact with industry and whose interests lie in their individual ambitions in science. In many LDCs, where over-educated scientists have difficulty in obtaining suitable research jobs, and most scientific activities are confined to educational institutions, the urge for unrestricted research funding is predominant. In many cases, this attitude reflects self-interest. As industrialization progresses, the need for applied scientists and engineers grows and the scientific community broadens its frontiers beyond the academic circle. It is natural that scientists in rapidly industrializing nations accept more practical views of science and technology.

In view of scientists' preference for unrestricted support by the state for scientific activities, development planners have been reluctant to provide special consideration for the development of science and technology. They consider science a cultural activity, and technology as only one component of economic development. Advocates of rapid economic development are reluctant to postpone economic growth in order to allow growth of domestic science and technology. To them, the value of a fully-operating indigenous technological system is secondary, and economic development may continue without a functioning domestic "full-cycle" science and technology system (from research to marketing). Their view is strong in many developing and developed countries that have relied on foreign technology and foreign training.

The STPI project did not accept either the liberal science view or the growth advocates' view. The contribution science and technology make to industrialization is too big to leave scientific and technological activities unprogrammed. The coupling between the scientific community and industry should be enhanced. To ignore the local scientists and engineers in decision-making would sacrifice a major national resource for economic development. Although foreign technology would play an important role in industrialization, the domestic technological system should do so also. In fact, one of the main policy issues that persisted in the STPI project was how to balance the utilization of foreign technology with local S&T inputs. The balancing act should be applied from the stage of assessment, employment, adaptation and regeneration of any modern technology that is introduced to industry for the first time.

In long-term economic development, technological development is an essential element, so that even in a short-term investment project technical implications must be given at least minimum consideration. This view, widely shared by technocrats, scientists and engineers involved in investment projects, is termed the "techno-economic" view. It is understandable that STPI members appreciated the value of this view. In the techno-economic view, decision-makers must be able to see beyond the individual industrialization project and its immediate effects. The potential of transferring imported technology horizontally to other users in the country must be taken into account whether or not the importer's interest may lie in its dissemination. If a technology has the potential for proliferation and generating modified technologies, it should be strongly considered. The spin-off effects are extremely desirable for LDCs. Also important is the match-up with existing scientific and technological capabilities. If a particular S&T capability exists and an imported technology has a high regenerative potential, the impact of the technology importation would be very high. (A good example is the commercial importation of solid-state electronic technology into Japan. Japan maximized the utilization of technology through subsequent R&D work by an increasing local S&T capability.)

During the STPI project, country teams presented case studies in which techno-economic views have made substantial contributions. These case studies helped STPI members in making assessments of policy options. Because of the wide variations in economic conditions and development strategies, case studies are much more practical than any normative approach. Undoubtedly, to techno-economists, international collaboration among LDC decision-makers is a strong instrument. As industrialization reaches a level at which the market must expand beyond national boundaries, and the technical content outweighs unskilled labour and facility-related capital, industrial decisions require evaluations of comparable decisions made by others in similar situations.

TECHNICAL COLLABORATION AMONG COUNTRIES

From the start of the STPI project, the search for collaborative mechanisms in the technological development of LDCs was a major theme. STPI researchers also considered the issue of technological self-reliance as a leading one in technology policy. It was inevitable that the STPI project should look into the historical relationships between the North and the South. Science is universal and technology is transacted between nations. Science and technology policy must contain elements of international relations and collaborative mechanisms.

The general North-South relationships in science and technology undergo several stages of development. When a developing country is in a very early stage, there is little significance to the S&T trade. Some LDC students are sent abroad for advanced training but their roles after their return to their native country are very limited. The government's attitude toward science and technology is neutral and without any specific aims. Superficial relationships exist with developed countries. As the LDC makes some progress in industrialization and economic development, the value of science and technology starts to attract the attention of decision-makers. They become fascinated by the wonders of modern technological civilization and soon adopt an open-door policy to science and technology. Any propositions to improve the S&T system are welcome, and developed countries are considered as suppliers of needed S&T knowledge. This liberal stage is followed by a painful recognition of the cost paid to acquire technology from the North. Decision-makers in LDCs are particularly bewildered by the hidden costs and restrictions imposed by technology suppliers. Many LDCs are now in this stage and there are numerous reports and studies on economic exploitation through technology. Nationalism in technology is the new catch-phrase. Many STPI countries were in this stage and a large number of STPI researchers could not escape their strong feelings against the tactics of multinationals and Northern technology suppliers.

It is a tribute to the STPI network that the intense discussion of technological exploitation and undesirable relationships between North and South was quickly followed up by a search of policy guidelines and instruments for organized technological trade between North and South. While LDCs strengthen their local technological capability, they have to rely on foreign technology. By judiciously selecting technologies and effectively disseminating them to local users, the economic benefits to the nation can be greatly enhanced. Furthermore, the roles of local scientists and engineers can become extremely useful by proper assignment of duties in this process. A lack of proper roles for local scientists and engineers is a result of unorganized S&T policies. In fact, enhanced importation of foreign technology can *increase* the roles of local scientists and engineers.

The ultimate goal of LDCs in the international technological system is to become "equal partners" in technological trade. No nation is going to be a technologically self-sufficient, isolated entity. The frontier of science and technology is too broad and, by its very nature, new scientific and technological advances defy a closed national boundary. Therefore, active technological transactions do exist among the Northern nations, and these transactions are conducted with mutual respect and balanced equity. LDCs are striving for equal partnership in the international S&T community. This achievement requires a matured national S&T system. This achievement cannot be attained through political dealings. Some STPI countries have shown remarkable progress in developing their S&T systems. In a short time, some STPI countries made the transition from an early indifferent attitude toward S&T to an organized technical trade stage. Yet no STPI country is in a position to conduct technological diplomacy with the North. However, history shows that many other nations have entered into technological diplomacy successfully, and there is no reason to believe that many LDCs cannot make it eventually.

The question whether technological diplomacy can be conducted among LDCs at a lower level of technical sophistication is a very interesting one. If LDCs can develop a forum through which limited technological exchange among LDCs may be conducted, it might create an environment that would foster a new type of technological development separate from the historical technical development of the North. The challenge is that there could be a different technical system from that of the North. This challenge is significant since many people question the merit of the current technical civilization of the North. Although it is an important question, the STPI network was not able to consider this issue adequately. But it is a stimulating policy question that must be dealt with by an international group.

The clear message of the STPI project is that confrontation between North and South is unnecessary and should be replaced by diplomacy. The STPI project also showed consistently that technical collaboration among LDCs could be much more beneficial. For example, technical managers of advanced LDCs have first-hand experience in initiating highly technical industrial projects in the LDC environment, whereas technical managers from developed countries have a difficult time understanding local conditions and constraints in LDCs. LDC engineers are more inclined to improvise to suit local conditions.

Because of the desirability of sharing techno-economic experience among LDC engineers and policymakers, the STPI project incorporated dissemination activities as an integral part of the project.

DISSEMINATION EFFORTS

Soon after the international synthesis meeting at Sussex, the dissemination activities of the STPI project were planned and conducted. More than 200 separate reports and documents were generated by the STPI project. Two documents are particularly useful for an overview of the project: *Methodological Guidelines for the STPI Project* (IDRC-067e) and *Main Comparative Report of the STPI Project* (IDRC-109e) by F. Sagasti and published by the IDRC.

Workshops are particularly important dissemination activities since the result of an action-oriented research is history itself. There was no way to recount the major STPI accomplishments in reports alone. Workshops conducted in an informal atmosphere turned out to be a very effective means for disseminating STPI results.

The first workshop was held at Kericho, Kenya, and was attended by S&T planners from English-speaking African nations. Most were high-ranking science policymakers and prominent policy analysts who have been extensively exposed to the international science policy community. The workshop was conducted in an informal way. Those associated with the STPI project encouraged critical comments from the participants, who had considerable experience in running their S&T systems. As with other STPI meetings held previously, the dissemination workshop became a forum of mutual learning.

The STPI project did not take up S&T manpower development as the major issue. At the Kericho workshop the participants repeatedly emphasized manpower development as the cornerstone of their S&T policies. With a unanimous voice the African participants valued the STPI work highly and even proposed the local African STPI network extend the project in the African environment.

The next workshop was held at Baguio City in the Philippines and the participants were from the Asian countries. Since many Asian nations are in the midst of rapid industrialization, the STPI reports were received with intense interest. The workshop was again conducted in an informal atmosphere and the exchange of case studies enhanced the formal presentations by the STPI reporters.

The third workshop was attended by S&T policymakers from the Arab world. Most participants were high-ranking government officials who were deeply involved in planning activities in their countries. The workshop resembled the early STPI meetings in the sense that the North-South confrontation was a major focus of discussion. These countries have the working capital for industrialization, and the determination to apply the correct policy measures for rapid industrialization was clearly expressed by the participants. STPI views were scrutinized closely and some alternative views were presented.

Workshops are planned for Latin-American countries and other LDCs not yet covered by the STPI disseminating efforts. It is appropriate that the STPI activities will continue in coming years, and that actions originated by the STPI project will continue.

The STPI project was only a beginning in the effort to integrate S&T policies with industrial activities. By no means did it complete its original mandate. The original scope of the work was too ambitious to be completed in a few years by several LDC research teams. The STPI project was an experiment, and the experiment has been shown to be a pioneering and rich experience for the participants. It can be argued in fact that the project has become a key factor in the future evolution of technical development in the participating countries. Only history will show us the magnitude of the impact created by the project. But all STPI participants would agree that it broadened their views of science and technology, industrialization and the developmental process.

CHAPTER FIVE

THE ANDEAN EXAMPLE

SALVADOR LLUCH SOLER

The STPI project is described in the previous chapter. This chapter deals with the Latin American focus of that project, which was carried out by Andean Pact nations. In addition to providing funds for the study of policy instruments, the IDRC grants made it possible to begin the actual implementation of two technological development projects, one on copper hydrometallurgy and one on the improved use of tropical woods.

 SALVADOR LLUCH SOLER is external assessor for the United Nations Industrial Development Organization in Lima, Peru. A civil engineer, he founded and directed the department of technological investigation at the Catholic University of Chile and later was director of the Chilean Steel Institute. Dr Lluch Soler was chief of the Chilean delegation that negotiated the Cartagena Agreement that led to the Andean Pact, and is one of the three members of the junta of the Andean Group of Nations.

T HE ANDEAN GROUP OF NATIONS, composed of the signatories to the Cartagena Agreement (Bolivia, Colombia, Ecuador, Peru and Venezuela), came into existence as the result of a joint effort aimed at permitting the capacities and potential of each participating nation to be used for the common good. The urgent task of raising living standards will be easier for each nation in the degree to which the capacity of the whole group is placed at the service of all, especially the weakest members.

Although the group has set itself specific quantitative and chronological goals, the scope of the undertaking is not limited. Its stated objectives have the nature of a framework-agreement allowing a broad range of activities to be undertaken through joint action.

A search for a common policy in the field of learning is proposed under the Cartagena Agreement. Article 25 states that one of the joint goals is to "achieve better use of scientific and technological progress, and to encourage research in these areas". On speaking of a common approach to foreign investment (Article 26) the existence of a coherent subregional technological policy is assumed.

But the statements included in the agreement are only an initial expression of the possible range of joint action in this field. It was only when the Andean Group began to operate and its basic apparatus had been installed, and after the agreement had begun to generate decisive joint action, that it was possible to glimpse the extent of both the commitment and the range of possibilities that joint action could lead to in the field of learning.

In addition, when the "Junta" (the technical body of the group) prepared proposals for a joint development strategy, an important factor became clear: the amount of modern technology that a nation possesses is a major determinant of its capacity for progress. It was also made clear that in our day and circumstances, modern technology is no longer the result of the work of the individual genius, but instead is achieved through collective decisions that can be deliberately organized. And above all, technology is both the source and the consequence of power.

The joint progress that the Andean subregions sought required that a workable mechanism be found to permit member countries to use their joint capacity to increase their limited individual capacities for technological progress, and to achieve this consciously, as the result of a choice between several equally valid alternatives.

BASES FOR A POLICY

To achieve a reasonably complete view of the problems involved, an intense and systematic effort was required that would not have been possible without the generous and timely support of the International Development Research Centre, and to a somewhat lesser, but also important extent, of the Organization of the American States.

This support allowed a series of studies to be conducted on a worldwide level, aimed at obtaining an extremely pragmatic and in-depth definition of the elements involved in forming a technological policy for the subregion. A detailed analysis was conducted in five countries (Italy, Yugoslavia, Japan, Czechoslovakia and Poland) of sectoral and national policies, of the activities of official institutions involved in science and technology and of the instruments they employ, especially in controlling the import of technology. A further parallel study was conducted in India, Holland and Sweden, aimed at examining the structure and technological alternatives of certain specific productive sectors.

The metallurgical sector was chosen for an in-depth study of specific experiences in searching for and obtaining technology internationally. The study was conducted in Mexico, Japan, India, Italy, Spain, Germany and Sweden.

An analysis of what was occurring in the Andean subregion itself was added to these studies, which were aimed at learning from foreign experience. An evaluation was made of existing research institutes, national policies in the area, available engineering consultant capacity, and information systems.

This ample background material permitted the Committee of the Cartagena Agreement to establish wide-ranging "bases for a subregional technological policy" in its Decision No. 84 (early June 1974). This aimed at promoting a continuous effort to acquire technological knowledge, and to improve the capacity to use it "keeping in mind the determining influence that it has on the orientation of economic and social development, and the opportunity it gives countries to act in an independent fashion in the international community".

The ideas contained in this Decision are extremely complex, and therefore difficult to summarize. Nevertheless, it is both possible and useful to point out some of the most important features:

1. The Decision deals with starting points from which gradual advancement can be achieved in areas considered to be of high priority due to their socio-economic importance.

2. The above presupposes the coordination and, in certain cases, the programming of scientific and technological activities at the regional level.

3. Joint action should encourage and protect regional technology; evaluate and control imported technology, and at the same time, facilitate the copying, assimilation and adaptation of foreign technology.

4. Special emphasis is placed on the fact that before any decisions on production are reached, the maximum range of alternative technologies should be considered, so as to be in a position to select the one that can be most profitably adapted to the nation in question.

5. It also emphasizes that technology is normally purchased in "packages" that can include either new or little-known techniques of a substantial character (in the Decision these are termed "seed" technologies) or simple and widely known technologies (called "peripheral"). It is obvious that the cost of the latter technologies could be substantially reduced or eliminated altogether, if the purchaser, when dealing with a specific project, is able and willing to discriminate between each category.

6. The above comments outline a concept underlining all aspects of Andean Group policy: that it is necessary to demythologize technology, and to view it as something that can be bought, sold, copied (and even stolen), and can be managed in accordance with more or less rational attitudes. It is clearly advisable (and always possible to a certain extent) to attempt to build up a national capacity for creation, dissemination, and production of technologies.

7. The policies of the Andean Group are not limited to recommending types of action and joint positions, but instead form a program for progressive action on the import and assimilation of technology, its adaptation, the recovery of unused knowledge, and stimulation for the creation of national techniques. All this is based on continuous contact and exchange of experience, and on a collective system of information.

TECHNOLOGICAL DEVELOPMENT PROJECTS

Decision 84 of the Andean Group systematizes ideas that in many cases are not new. But it has the twin advantages of being a coherent approach covering a wide range of problems, and the product of both careful theoretical analysis and of international experience that it was possible to compile directly, thanks to the substantial support given by IDRC.

On the other hand, the program proposed in the Decision includes, among other measures, a plan of action that, at least insofar as developing countries are concerned, is a new contribution: the undertaking to implement the so-called Andean Technological Development Projects. These are activities intended to solve common problems through a joint effort that has been very carefully planned in regard to both its timetable and program of activities.

The development of these projects permits IDRC support to be duly evaluated. In addition to the support provided for establishing Andean Group policies and formulating various technological development projects, further assistance has been provided for implementing some of the projects themselves. Both aspects contribute to the establishment of channels through which contributions from other sources of aid are funnelled.

Two projects were begun: the work on copper hydrometallurgy, and the studies on the improved use of tropical woods. Both subjects are of critical importance for one or more countries of the subregion.

THE COPPER PROJECT

Bolivia and Peru have large deposits of copper-bearing minerals. Of special interest is the waste that has accumulated over the years from other mining operations such as tin mining. These large deposits of waste contain a small amount of copper, which would be worth a considerable sum if techniques could be developed to permit the metal to be recovered at low cost.

In addition, use of modern hydrometallurgical methods would also permit recovery of low-grade or low-density deposits which at present do not justify the heavy investments that would be required if other procedures were used. Therefore, it seemed attractive to train technicians from both countries in the use of hydrometallurgical processes of three types: bonding with scrap iron; electro-ionization replacement; and the newest and most promising, which is bacterial leaching.

A detailed program of activities was drawn up as part of the initial project included in the technological policies of the Andean Group, which received substantial financial support from IDRC. This program provided for the training of a group of technicians from both countries. The training was to begin with theoretical studies on the above-mentioned procedures, and progress by steps through the laboratory stage up to the industrial plant stage, including the basic and specialized engineering required to design the plant, and culminating in the construction itself. Therefore, the personnel were to receive training in specific projects that would progress up to the industrial stage.

It should be noted here that the program for technological development in copper production, prepared with IDRC support, received financial aid from the government of the Federal Republic of Germany for its continuation and completion, while IDRC and CIDA supported the project on tropical wood which is discussed below. This type of cooperation, in which one source of foreign aid complements and continues the work of another, permits long-range programs to be undertaken as well as sustained efforts in economic and technological development. The support of IDRC in setting up the overall policy and in the initial pilot projects permitted the subsequent activities, supported by Germany, to be built on a solid foundation with a high probability of success.

The program on copper hydrometallurgy was begun in January 1975. Much has been achieved in four years.

Plans for the construction of a copper oxide treatment plant with a capacity of 1,000 tons per day, to be built at Corocoro, Bolivia, have been completed. The engineering studies have been finished, and arrangements for financing the construction have been begun.

At Toromocho, Peru, a complex for producing copper solutions by means of bacterial leaching is now in production. The metal is recovered through bonding with scrap iron at a plant that was also designed locally.

In connection with these projects, specialized training and upgrading was provided for a group of 23 professionals from both countries, who worked in a complementary fashion performing some activities in common and some specialized activities. Some support personnel, such as draftsmen, etc., also received training.

Because the plants were designed locally, considerable financial savings were made. Direct and thorough knowledge of the processes and the conditions affecting the location, permits large sums to be saved without affecting efficiency or quality. It is possible to take advantage of the installed capacity of the country to construct certain equipment and, above all, to replace costly imported material with cheaper and more easily obtainable material.

A noteworthy case is the use of wood instead of stainless steel in the construction of the walls of the deposits for holding copper solutions. Another is the use of gravity instead of pumping systems, which was achieved by arranging the deposits at regular intervals on natural inclines.

The design itself, its adaptation to local conditions and the purchase of parts within the country have had economic consequences that, in the case of the plant at Corocoro can be expressed in the following rough figures: a plant having a 600-ton-per-day capacity designed abroad would have cost $12 million (the lowest offer); the development of the project under discussion permitted a plant with a 1,000-ton-per-day capacity to be built for about the equivalent of $7.2 million. Taking into consideration the effects that local construction will have during the operating stage, the economic advantage is even greater.

It is not possible to evaluate the economic significance of bacterial leaching in low-grade deposits. However, it is illuminating to point out that in 1976 when the project was prepared, it was estimated that the techniques to be used would allow, in the case of waste from former mines alone, an amount to be recovered that would reach $130 million in the case of Peru and $80 million in the case of Bolivia (1973 dollars).

THE TROPICAL WOODS PROJECT

An initial analysis indicated the great importance to the Andean subregion of obtaining more information on tropical woods, permitting this resource to be rationally exploited and used to meet urgent and varied social needs.

The tropical forests of the Andean Group cover more than 50 percent of their total physical area and contain approximately 36 billion cubic metres of usable wood. Nevertheless, present use of this immense resource does not amount to even 0.1 percent per year, and contributes a mere 5 percent to the agricultural product of the member countries. In addition, in most cases the forests cover lands unsuitable for other uses. Finally, present exploitation involves extremely rudimentary techniques.

Wood technology is based on the characteristics of conifers and other temperate-climate species, which have been known and used since ancient times. These species are relatively few in number, and those used for construction are relatively homogeneous. Tropical wood is very different. For example, temperate-climate woods vary in density from approximately 0.30 to 0.50 gr/cm^3 and the more than 2,500 species of tropical woods existing in the forests of the Andean Group vary in density from 0.10 to almost 1.20 gr/cm^3.

Although some research into forest resources was being conducted at the national level, there was no systematic activity covering the entire subregion, nor any suitably uniform methodologies for comparing the results. It was therefore necessary to undertake a joint project, oriented in its first stage to the study of the physical, chemical, and preservational properties of a substantial number of species, duly identified and classified. IDRC provided substantial new contributions to this study, to which support from CIDA was added.

In the first stage of the project more than 100,000 tests were made on samples systematically collected from 105 forest species. (The most important species are included among the 2,500 mentioned above.) The physical and mechanical properties of these 105 species have been determined, as well as their individual response to drying and preservation, their workability, and their most suitable combinations — or their behaviour in various types of combination. This broad and extensive experimental work has produced the most important data bank in the world on tropical woods.

These studies permitted standards for the visual classification of cut tropical wood to be prepared, and an Andean system for classifying structural wood to be established that separates the species studied into three groups according to their resistance characteristics.

The Andean Laboratory for Wood Engineering was set up in Lima to serve the five countries. It has facilities to test life-size structural elements, and is constructing a system for seismic simulation that will determine the behaviour of houses or other wooden or mixed structures in cases of dynamic stress.

Using this large amount of information the *Andean Manual on Wood Structural Designs* was prepared: the first publication on tropical woods to achieve this level of coverage and detail. Based on the manual and all other available information, two simplified and more widely distributed booklets were also published, one for users and the other for educational purposes.

More than 40 technicians from the five participating countries have been trained, and in addition national agencies in charge of forestry policies have been persuaded to give due importance to the technological aspects implicit in their activities. In some cases, as in Ecuador and Bolivia for example, work in wood technology was non-existent or extremely rudimentary; the project has permitted wood technology to be introduced or strengthened.

Wood technology is studied as part of the Andean Pact program.

CIDA has provided financing for setting up a wood technology laboratory at Santa Cruz, Bolivia.

Patterned methodologies and joint standards have been established so that it will be possible to compare and exchange the results of future work. Important advances have also been achieved in the design and manufacture of efficient and cheap testing equipment, including complicated equipment such as the vibrating system for dynamic tests.

Finally, and without exhausting the list of positive results, it should be noted that, in each of the participating countries, interdisciplinary inter-coordinated groups have been formed, made up of engineers, architects and other professionals who assist in extending the rational use of such an important and abundant natural resource at the same time as they cooperate in project activities.

A VIEW TO THE FUTURE

The research activities described above have shown that it is possible to obtain useful and concrete results that not only solve important problems but also generate the local capacity to continue similar efforts and to undertake additional ones. The path that has been successfully opened permits new, more important and far-reaching tasks to be undertaken.

The second stage of the tropical wood project will be implemented in the near future, and will be primarily directed toward the design of basic structures, above all housing. The experience gained will be extended and applied to the solution of one of the most serious problems faced by the countries of the Andes: the housing shortage. The fact that the total housing shortage in the five countries reaches a figure of approximately 1,225,000 units should serve to give some idea of the size of the problem.

The project has been planned to include a series of activities ranging from research on architectural and structural design to the planning of housing subdivisions, including the necessary socio-economic and climatological studies, so that the units will conform to the customs and economic level of their inhabitants, as well as the conditions of the geographic area where they are to be constructed.

An important financial contribution to the development of this second stage (more than $2.5 million) has been obtained from the Commission of European Communities. IDRC, whose support permitted the process to be begun, will also contribute, aiding in the completion of some aspects of the study of tropical wood that were not totally covered in the first stage.

NUTRITION STUDIES

Several studies conducted by national and international organizations point out that in our member countries calorie and protein dietary deficiencies affect more than 25 percent of the infant population in each nation, and in some cases the figure is as high as 65 percent. In addition to these figures on malnutrition, there are very high infant mortality rates varying from 51.7 to 78.5 per thousand live births for children under one year of age, and from 5.7 to 14.9 per thousand for children between the ages of one and four. Furthermore, clinical research conducted in the last ten years has demonstrated that protein deficiencies in the first months of life have an irreversible adverse effect on the neuro-motor and intellectual development of the child, seriously affecting his capacity to learn.

The above is one reason (and by no means the only one) for beginning a program that, by utilizing the different raw materials readily available in each zone, would make low-cost, nutritionally-balanced food available to low-income families. For different combinations of available raw materials, the planned activities include research on the processing and make-up of food products from the laboratory stage to the semi-industrial stage, and experimental introduction of these products into the institutional and commercial markets.

The goal is not only to prepare balanced foods, but also to ensure that they are acceptable, and to plan mechanisms for their distribution. The financing needed for this program has also been obtained from the Commission of European Communities. The plan of the project itself was financed by IDRC.

SPECIFIC PROGRAMMING

The Andean technological development projects, which represent some results of the overall policies discussed at the outset, conform to carefully prepared specific plans for obtaining equally specific results. These plans are carefully studied (the planning for the project on nutrition took more than four years of continuous work), and when they are implemented they are placed in the hands of the "contracting committee" appointed by the participating countries and the Junta of the Andean Group. This is a specific body created for each project that performs an overseeing function that can be compared to the role of a technically and economically skilled manager who takes charge of the construction of a building. The procedure in itself is not a new one, but it is new in this field in the majority of developing countries, where research activities, if they exist, often come to grief because they are too general.

CONCLUSION AND SUMMARY

In the above remarks, I have tried to describe the evolution of the program developed by the Andean Group with the so-often-mentioned co-operation of IDRC, and that of CIDA, OAS, the Government of the Federal

Republic of Germany, and the Commission of European Communities. It would be useful to list some of the conclusions that can be drawn from the successful development of this program:

1. Advances in learning can and should be planned, as is the case in many other human activities.

2. The aid received from IDRC permitted the countries of the Andes to develop a global, organic plan that, utilizing world-wide experience, was adapted to the special conditions of the subregion.

3. This overview permitted coherent policies to be developed, aimed at gradually making national structures and decisions more responsive to the challenge (and the opportunities) of world-wide technological progress.

4. The policy adopted includes various modes of action, among which the Andean technological development programs stand out. IDRC support permitted the first programs to be developed and allowed one of them to be implemented. The first two programs (the other, as has been mentioned, was financed by the Federal Republic of Germany) showed that, with a deliberate effort, it is possible to achieve important progress in complex technical problems, even in countries lacking experience and having a weak infrastructure.

5. The generous and open-minded attitude of the agency that was our initial sponsor made it easier for other bodies providing international aid to join in the effort. The resulting multinational cooperation permitted the scope and depth of the work to be greatly increased. The IDRC's substantial contribution was the necessary catalyst.

6. It is interesting to examine the sequence in which the Andean technological development projects were formulated. Without sacrificing continuity, we have passed from activities directed toward better utilization of basic resources to other activities that, although related to the former, are aimed instead at meeting the primary requirements of the neediest sectors of society. This direction was the result of the normal course of events, and demonstrates the extent to which communal action, of which joint technological policy is a very vivid expression, has carved out its own path based on the present reality of Andean society.

CHAPTER SIX

BASIS FOR A BLUE REVOLUTION?

QUITERIO FAJARDO MIRAVITE

In 1977, scientists at the Southeast Asian Fisheries Development Centre (SEAFDEC) in the Philippines became the first anywhere to succeed in breeding milkfish (*Chanos chanos*) in captivity. The advance was made possible by an IDRC grant, approved in 1974, for a three-year project of research in the breeding and rearing of this important source of protein. The initial grant, for $826,000, was renewed for another three years in December 1978 in the amount of $421,100.

 QUITERIO FAJARDO MIRAVITE is the executive
director of the aquaculture department of SEAFDEC,
at Tigbauan, Iloilo, Philippines, which he played a
large part in establishing. A graduate of universities in
both the Philippines and India, Dr Miravite has had a
wide-ranging career in the course of which he has
been journalist, editor, teacher and acting university
president. He has travelled widely in his studies of
fisheries and aquaculture.

A LONG THE SHORES of many of the islands dotting the Philippine Archipelago, one can often see men, women and even children patiently pushing a triangular bamboo and net contraption in waist-deep water, as if winnowing the seas in a timeless fashion. Now and then they stop to scoop something out of the small end of the net with a small plate into a pail or basin. To an untrained eye the catch is all but invisible. A closer look reveals hundreds of tiny black dots occasionally darting in the water. The "dots" are actually the eyes of hundreds of tiny, as yet transparent, milkfish fry.

More than a billion fry with a value of at least US$8 million are now caught annually with at least 170,000 individuals directly or indirectly dependent on the industry. If as a result of some ecological catastrophe the milkfish fry supply should suddenly disappear, the Philippine aquaculture industry would simply collapse because the milkfish fry catch is the backbone of the industry.

For this reason, the Aquaculture Department of the Southeast Asian Fisheries Development Center (SEAFDEC) launched a program to conduct studies on the milkfish, with the major objective of stabilizing fry production. In June 1975 the program was given a big boost with the approval of a three-year grant from the International Development Research Centre amounting to $826,000. Since then the program has amassed scientific data on the biology of the milkfish and has scored a global breakthrough that augurs well for the milkfish farming industry.

THE MILKFISH

Bangus, as the milkfish is popularly known in the Philippines, is a remarkable species in many ways. Known in science as *Chanos chanos*, it belongs taxonomically to the family Chanidae of which it is the sole living member. Fossil relatives of the milkfish have been found in European cretaceous and eocene deposits. The beautiful silvery fish with its streamlined, moderately compressed spindle-shaped body is the product of evolutionary processes, hence its hardiness and adaptability to differing environmental conditions. It is distributed widely within the tropical and subtropical area of the Pacific and Indian Oceans; spanning the waters on both the east and west coasts of Africa, North and Central America; from the Southern coast of Japan to the north, and down to Australia in the south. The land mass and the frigid Antarctic waters have apparently barred it from colonizing the Atlantic, since there has been no report on the species from the Atlantic Ocean.

Milkfish can survive and grow in waters fresh enough to be drinkable as well as in waters with up to three times as much salt as regular seawater, such as is found in island lagoons in the Pacific. They can, in fact, stay alive in ponds where the high salt content has killed most other fish, and withstand temperatures considerably higher than those that could occur in their natural habitat.

The dietary needs of the milkfish are simple. They are primarily vegetarian and subsist on minute benthic and planktonic organisms as well as decayed plant materials submerged in water. Animal organisms are consumed by the milkfish only as an incidental admixture to the main vegetable part of the diet. Because of its feeding habit, the milkfish can be considered an aquatic analog of the cow. It does not require artificially compounded feed and can be produced in large quantities by using only the natural food that grows on pond bottoms.

Marketable milkfish range in size from 200 to 400 grams. This size range can be attained in from two to six months depending upon the cultural practice used. In well-managed ponds, a production rate of 2,000 kg per hectare per year is easily attainable.

With its ability to withstand environmental extremes, its simple feeding requirements and its fast growth rate, the milkfish lends itself to controlled husbandry or culture. Its distribution, encompassing the tropical and semi-tropical regions of the globe, in which are found many developing countries with their long-recognized protein deficiencies, make milkfish an ideal, cheap protein source for the masses.

However, they have one major drawback: they are not known to spawn in captivity. Milkfish farmers have to continually obtain wild fry as seed stock. The milkfish that are marketed are only in their early juvenile stage. Adult milkfish, known as sabalo in the Philippines, are at least 85 cm long, weigh more than 6 kg and are at least 4 years old. When ripe, a female milkfish can bear more than three million eggs. Because of this, the Philippine government has placed an absolute ban on the capture and sale of sabalo.

ECONOMIC STATUS AND POTENTIAL

At present there are only three places where milkfish are cultured on a large scale: the Philippines, Taiwan and Indonesia. Of these three, Taiwan has the smallest area devoted to milkfish, with only 15,624 ha, but has the highest annual productivity at 2,000 kg per ha. Indonesia has the largest pond area available, with 184,609 ha, but it is also the least productive at 358 kg per ha per year. The Philippines has 176,032 ha of fishponds, of which 90 percent is utilized for milkfish, with an average annual productivity of 580 kg per ha. In addition the rich waters of Laguna de Bay, the Philippines largest freshwater lake, are also utilized for the culture of milkfish in pens: some 6,000 ha of fishpens are in operation there. In the fishpen, an annual productivity of 10 tons per ha is attainable. Altogether, the combined investments in Taiwan, Indonesia and the Philippines are valued at US$600 to $1,000 million, producing a total of 200 million kg annually.

This production estimate is nowhere near the potential capability of the entire Asia-Pacific region. Indonesia has 3 million ha of mangrove and the Philippines 400,000 ha with potential for milkfish production. All in all in Asia and the Pacific region, some 6 million ha of mangrove are potential milkfish producing areas. It may not be ecologically sound to develop all the mangroves for aquaculture. However, if even a quarter of this area should be made available for milkfish culture, and assuming only a very low annual productivity of 500 kg per ha, some 750 million kg could be produced. Together with production from existing ponds, close to one million tonnes of milkfish could be realized per year.

Milkfish production is a labour-intensive operation. It is estimated that the manpower requirement for operating a milkfish pond is one person per hectare. Thus, opening 1.5 million ha within the region will employ 1.5 million people. This figure does not include manpower requirement for construction and development as well as fry collection.

Milkfish constitute 10 percent of the fish produced in the Philippines, with a total volume of 113,194 tonnes. Without developing new ponds, by merely doubling the present productivity of milkfish ponds using improved methods, an increment equal to the present production can be attained. A very modest export in milkfish also exists, fluctuating between 52 and 151 tonnes from 1971 to 1975, with a total value ranging from P0.666 to P1.186 million. The export caters mainly to Filipinos living in the United States. There is no reason why the market for de-boned milkfish cannot be expanded outside the traditional ethnic market, since the fish has a delicate flavour.

If harvested and canned in small sizes of 10 to 15 cm, the milkfish could compete well with sardines which the Asian and Pacific region still import in large quantities. Asians traditionally rely on fish rather than meat as their chief protein source. With proper preparation there is no reason why milkfish cannot be acceptable anywhere in the Asian and Pacific region.

Another market for small milkfish is as live bait for tuna fishing as practised by Taiwanese and Japanese fleets. Milkfish can readily be held in live tanks at high densities — a characteristic important for use as live bait. However, in these last two forms of marketing the product hinges on the availability of more fry.

TECHNOLOGICAL GAP IN MILKFISH FARMING

The relatively low productivity of ponds in the Philippines and Indonesia compared with those of Taiwan is not due to the lack of technology: the technology for intensive culture exists. In the Philippines a few pond operators routinely harvest 2,000 kg per ha per year. One progessive farmer has in fact devised a new system of culture capable of yielding two tonnes per ha per crop with five crops a year, or a total annual productivity of ten tonnes per ha.

A program to disseminate currently available technology to milkfish producers, coupled with financing, technical and extension services, could easily double or treble present average productivity. Seminars and training sessions for pond operators and caretakers need to be organized. Technical service laboratories for soil and water analysis, strategically located in major fishpond areas, will be essential for trouble-shooting purposes, in order to back up the recommendation of extension workers. A cur-

Catching milkfish fry in nets was until recently the only way to supply fish farmers.

rent study estimates that 15 percent of the fry die from the time they are caught to the time they are stocked, while another 54 percent die during the rearing period. Improvement of pond practices to the level now enjoyed by the progessive farmers will result in a greater number of harvestable fish, even with the same volume of fry catch.

Despite the sophistication that exists in milkfish rearing in ponds, one undeniable fact remains — the industry is totally dependent on the acquisition of fry from the wild. The natural supply of fry, while probably adequate with the present level of demand, is highly unstable and subject to the vagaries of forces beyond man's control and total comprehension, even with the aid of modern science. As environmental degradation takes place with increasing industrialization, it is hard to predict how much longer the present fry supply can be sustained. Furthermore, as fish farmers improve their skills, enabling them to stock more fry per unit area, the total demand can be expected to rise correspondingly.

It is therefore imperative to fully domesticate the milkfish in order to have total control over its entire life cycle. And milkfish can only be considered fully domesticated when man is able to obtain mature milkfish in captivity, spawn them at will, and produce the fry under controlled conditions. The production of milkfish fry in hatcheries could then augment the natural supply and at the same time serve as a back-up in case of ecological catastrophe.

Unfortunately, despite the milkfish's widespread abundance and recognized utility, its life cycle remains shrouded in mystery. Full understanding of its biology will be essential for full domestication. This requires painstaking research and sustained support to carry out basic studies. The interest has always been high. Attempts to spawn milkfish have been made for some years in the Philippines, Indonesia, Taiwan and Hawaii. However, none of these efforts were backed by sustained support and consequently could not be carried out on the scale necessary.

THE MILKFISH PROJECT

In answer to the need for a sustained and concerted effort in milkfish research, especially in seed production, the SEAFDEC Aquaculture Department in Tigbauan, Iloilo Province on the island of Panay (Philippines), with the financial assistance of the IDRC, embarked on a research program on a scale never before attempted.

The milkfish project was conceived with the following objectives:

1. Ensure an adequate and reliable supply of milkfish fry, in addition to those collected from natural sources, and extend and stabilize the period of fry availability throughout the year involving domestication and breeding of adult fish;

2. Develop economically and nutritionally effective feeds from local sources for juvenile stages of fish while evolving improved methods of pond culture and management, including pond engineering and polyculture with shrimp and other compatible species;

3. Provide the means for required overseas and local training of researchers as well as short-term training for milkfish pond operators, technicians and extension workers; and

4. Determine, assess and alleviate critical socio-economic constraints in the entire structure of the milkfish aquaculture industry while controlling biological factors of predation and disease, and evaluate the profitability and effects of innovations.

The project started virtually from scratch. There was very little known about milkfish except for some early morphological studies. The last and only description of milkfish eggs and larvae was made in 1929 by a Dutch scientist, Dr H.C. Delsman. The scientists in the project were faced with questions that were very basic in nature. For instance, where and how do you catch a sabalo alive and having caught one, how do you keep the adult milkfish alive in captivity? How do you handle a 6-10 kg fish that thrashes about excitedly without injuring it? How do you distinguish the male from the female? What do you feed the captive sabalo? Most important, what kind of hormone or hormones — and how much — should you use to induce spawning?

During initial attempts, the adult milkfish, once captured, rarely lasted more than two or three days. The transparent, imperforate, adipose eyelids covering the eye became cloudy and the fish swam around blindly, inflicting more injuries on themselves and finally dying. In captivity they were highly excitable and would jump out of the water when they detected the slightest movement outside the water.

The site for the milkfish station, like most rural areas in the Philippines, was languid and unhurried. But with the onset of the program it was to become the scene of the most frenetic efforts in the history of Philippine science. The site was selected primarily because of the existence there of a giant, fixed net known by its Japanese name, *otoshi-ami*, where adult milkfish are caught with the least injury. Furthermore, the province of Antique is the Philippines' major milkfish fry collecting ground. During the 1976 spawning season 259 adult milkfish were collected of which 19 percent died of injuries sustained during capture and transport.

Capturing the fish involved their transfer from the *otoshi-ami* to a transport cage made of PVC and nylon net, then to shore in an outrigged motor boat and finally to a 1.5-meter-long plastic bag on the shore. While inside the plastic cocoon filled with water, the fish were rushed in a stretcher to large tanks made of rubberized canvas. The tendency of the milkfish's eyelids to cloud up was checked by subjecting the fish to low salinity water during the first 10 to 20 days of captivity. In this manner a stock of breeders was collected and tamed for experimental manipulation.

PROJECT ACCOMPLISHMENTS

During the 1976 spawning season, 16 sabalo were injected with purified salmon gonadotropin. Two females responded to the treatment, ovulated and produced hydrated eggs. Unfortunately none of the males responded to the treatment; thus there was no sperm available for fertilization.

Finally on April 15, 1977, the first artificial fertilization of milkfish eggs, a world breakthrough, was achieved. The fertilized eggs were incubated and the resulting larvae successfully reared to fingerling stage. Out of a few thousand fertilized, only 37 reached the fingerling stage. Survival was low, but the experiment proved that milkfish could be bred in captivity. During the 1978 season, the number of fry carried through the larval stage was considerably higher: 38,000. The fingerlings so produced are now being reared in earthen ponds at the department's Leganes station.

All the successful spawning experiments were conducted using milkfish that were already mature when captured. This merely pushes back the hunting phase from fry to spawner collection. Obviously a hatchery has to have a more reliable supply of spawners than what can be caught by chance in the open sea. This being the case the major thrust is now on inducing maturation in pond-grown milkfish while larval rearing techniques are being refined for mass production. A captive broodstock is now kept in special pens constructed in the sheltered cover at the SEAFDEC's Igang station in Guimaras island, off Panay; this will be utilized for experiments on induced maturation.

In the course of the studies on the breeding of captive milkfish, several peripheral but essential findings were also achieved. External morphological differences between male and female have been discovered in the anal region, thus making it possible to distinguish sex without injury to the fish. The infestation by an external parasite, Caligus, was found to be controllable with use of a chemical agent, Neguvon. Several spawning areas have been identified around the island of Panay. Valuable preliminary data on the swimming behaviour and movements of the sabalo were obtained using ultrasonic tagging. Age of the breeders has been determined using patterns of lines in the scales as indicators. Food and feeding habits of the sabalo were determined by stomach content analysis.

Studies on pond cultivation have not focused on technological innovation per se, since as mentioned earlier the culture techniques now employed by some progressive milkfish farmers are already very sophisticated. However, it is imperative that those techniques already developed be standardized for dissemination to other farmers. In order for the techniques to be applicable and adaptable to any pond situation, it is essential to know the basic relationships between soil and water condition and the growth of natural food organisms in the pond. With this knowledge, essential technical services can be designed to help the fish farmers. Only then can the technology be tailored to suit to the conditions peculiar to each pond.

Parallel to the scientific studies, socio-economic studies were also conducted on the milkfish industry. While extensive literature on the agricultural sector is available, no similar data for aquaculture exists. There was a dearth of knowledge on the target clientele for the project. Who they were, how much they earned, their aspirations, their problems — all these were painstakingly obtained through a nationwide survey of the aquaculture industry covering not only milkfish farmers and fry gatherers but also oyster and mussel farmers. The survey included the present techniques being used by the farmers and their productivity, which could serve as baseline data for assessing the effects of future technology dissemination.

PROJECT ASSESSMENT

The scientific breakthrough achieved in the project, namely the artificial fertilization of milkfish eggs, and subsequent success in rearing the larvae, will need further refinement before it can make a social and economic impact. Indeed, the breakthrough has proven that the objective of the project is attainable.

Because it is easy to raise and is widespread throughout the tropical world, the milkfish could become the miracle fish in a "blue revolution," and provide a vast new source of animal protein for the world's hungry masses.

For Asians, whose basic protein source is fish, the breakthrough becomes even more meaningful. Fish culture in general has been practised in Asia for many centuries. Milkfish culture in particular has been part of the socio-economic milieu of the Philippines for the past several hundred years. Although its origins are now lost, the fishpond is just as much an integral part of the Philippine scene as is the rice paddy.

The IDRC-funded milkfish project was the first major, serious effort to develop new technology for milkfish culture that went beyond merely improving pond productivity by addressing itself to the crucial problem of seed production. There had been numerous attempts to make milkfish spawn, but they were miniscule, sporadic and unsustained, and therefore failed. Thus it was to be expected that the breeding breakthrough would draw acclamation from both the press and industry, after an announcement by President Ferdinand E. Marcos.

Eventual mastery of the life cycle of the milkfish is expected to ensure an adequate, increasing and continuing supply of fry for a fishpond industry that has, since time immemorial, relied on the mercy and vagaries of nature for its source of wild stock.

Assurance of fry supply could eventually stabilize and expand the industry and stimulate the establishment of canning and other processing plants to absorb excess production for export. Vast tracts of undeveloped marshlands could be converted into productive ponds and generate employment while raising income levels in the rural countryside.

As a result of the breakthrough, aquaculture in the Philippines has been seen in a new and more important light, with greater emphasis now being placed on its role in national development. Budgetary support for the Philippine Bureau of Fisheries and Aquatic Resources, as well as for the SEAFDEC Aquaculture Department, has more than trebled over the past few years.

In a parallel development, the government has mounted a massive credit financing program for fisheries development to trigger a blue revolution, similar to the program for rice production which saw the country achieve sufficiency in this staple commodity within a few years. This development followed closely the visit in May 1978 of President Marcos to the SEAFDEC research station in Iloilo.

Although it is a multinational, regional organization, the department's accomplishments have been cited in the five-year economic development plan of the national government; in its integrated fisheries development component, research on milkfish has been entirely entrusted to the department.

National interest in fisheries development is likewise expressed in the plan establishing a state university with a basic fisheries thrust in the immediate vicinity of the department's main station in Iloilo. The new institution, which is part of the University of the Philippines System, will stimulate the growth, along with the SEAFDEC project, of a fish estate, much in the pattern of the rice estate that grew out of the University of the Philippines in Los Baños with its thrust in agriculture and the nearby International Rice Research Institute (IRRI).

As the milkfish breakthrough was achieved by local researchers and a Canadian scientist assigned to the project, it gave new and abounding national confidence in the capability of the Filipino as scientist. It has also attracted a number of Filipino scientists from abroad to return to their country and participate in milkfish research, to reverse, even in a modest way, the brain-drain process for the first time.

Milkfish research at SEAFDEC has likewise drawn the interest of other scientists in the field. Collaborative arrangements have been made with other research institutions in the United States, Indonesia, India, China and France, to exchange both information and expertise to hasten work on the milkfish, and facilitate technical cooperation among developed and developing economies.

But the success of the project lies as much to the well-defined objective and the enthusiasm of the participants involved as to the nature of the grant and its manner of implementation. It was awarded without any constraint as to nationality of the staff to be hired or the source of materials and equipment to be purchased. This acquisition of essential equipment and supplies was based purely on quality, economics and speed of delivery rather than on the country of manufacture.

The grant, one of the largest, if not the largest ever awarded for the study of one single species in the history of the Philippine fisheries, assumes a great significance due to its long-range objective and lasting impact. It is development-oriented, applied research with long-term goals that could be of tremendous assistance to developing countries. Altruism in foreign assistance programs is often suspect. But the IDRC grant on milkfish research to SEAFDEC cannot possibly be clouded by such doubts, because in no way will the progress in milkfish farming in Asia benefit Canadian economy.

CHAPTER SEVEN

AN AFRICAN FAMILY AFFAIR

KOFFI ATTIGNON

Few popular publications available to the mass of French-speaking West Africans deal seriously with such matters as family health, nutrition, hygiene, sexual education and family planning. Responding to the expressed need for a responsible yet appealing presentation of such information, the IDRC provided funds for the establishment of a new magazine called *Famille et Développement*. The magazine, run largely by Africans for Africans, has been a huge success. The project began in 1973 with a grant of $644,000. An additional grant of $264,000 was approved in 1977 to continue the publication and provide for its takeover by an autonomous, non-profit international organization.

 KOFFI ATTIGNON is director of the Village du Benin, a French-language school in Lome, Togo, for people from Commonwealth countries. A geographer, Dr Attignon has been secretary-general in Togo's ministry of education and scientific research for the past 10 years.

MOST OF THE SOLUTIONS planned to break the vicious cycle of underdevelopment are thwarted by a lack of awareness among those concerned. This acts like a negative catalyst to prevent the desired reaction from taking place. Once those involved are made aware of their situation, development will occur by leaps and bounds. This at any rate is the conclusion reached by some development experts.

Unless this condition is met, giving aid to the Third World will be like trying to fill a bucket with a hole in it: simply a waste of money, time and energy. When those involved are made aware, a little aid to the under-developed countries will go a long way. As the African proverb says, "With enough drops of water you can fill a jar."

Creation of awareness among those concerned will be the positive catalyst that will give impetus to the process of development. It will create among underdeveloped peoples a change of attitude that will end the passivity and resignation one always finds among those who receive handouts.

Instead of holding out their hands, they will roll up their sleeves and become the conscious, competent authors of their own development. Instead of scanning the horizon waiting for help from the other side of the Mediterranean or Atlantic, they will brandish their hoes, hammers, or pens to build a place to stand. Instead of becoming discouraged in the face of their needs, they will use what they have wisely to solve their problems.

In this way, rather than being their essential means of support, aid will become a supplementary source and will eventually no longer be necessary.

It is with this purpose in mind that the International Development Research Centre has provided aid to *Famille et Développement*, an African magazine for education in development. *Famille et Développement* proposes to inform Africans and increase their awareness in order that they may promote their own development.

One of the focal points of *Famille et Développement* is the family, the unit in which a man is born and raised. Every form of social development must have its roots in this social cell. Every activity performed in this nucleus, this social building-block, will have definite results on society as a whole. For this reason the themes dealt with in *Famille et Développement* concern every aspect of the family economy and its well-being: nutrition, hygiene, family planning, safety of the mother and child and so on.

The magazine's second focal point is development, that is, all of the sectors that contribute to development: education and the most suitable type of schools; rural development in all its complexity; handicaps to development such as the Third World arms race, and wasteful expenditures for prestige purposes.

THE "FAMILLE ET DEVELOPPEMENT" PROJECT

Under the auspices of the Quaker Service and the Mali Ministry of National Education, an international seminar was held in Bamako in April 1973 on Sex Education in Tropical Africa. The seminar included about 50 male and female African participants from 11 French-speaking African countries south of the Sahara. One of their recommendations was that a news magazine on family health problems should be established.

With the help of the IDRC, this ambition was realized in record time, to the great satisfaction of all involved. In December 1973, a committee met in Dakar to determine the general orientation this African magazine would have, and an editing committee was formed. Its members agreed to work as volunteers.

In November 1974 a pilot issue of *Famille et Développement* was published and regular publication began in January 1975. The magazine became a spectacular success, and it created a veritable revolution both in terms of the concept itself, the scientific validity and objectivity of its articles and its technical excellence: the paper was of exceptional quality and the illustrations were many and varied. Even more surprising was the fact that not one member of the *Famille et Développement* team, from the director and chief editor down to the members of the editorial committee, had any previous journalistic experience.

So resounding was the magazine's initial success that many jealously questioned whether this African family health magazine, edited in Africa by Africans, could survive the year. Even its most optimistic proponents did not feel that *Famille et Développement* could remain faithful to its original orientations, maintain the same level of technical quality and survive through 17 issues to January 1979. Indeed this would not have been possible without the generous support of the IDRC, which has provided the magazine with capital grants.

WHO THE MAGAZINE IS FOR

In theory, *Famille et Développement* is designed for all social classes, from the head of state to the peasant. There is something in the magazine for everybody, regardless of social rank.

There is a wealth of information in the magazine for upper management people, and it provides a forum for the exchange of practical information. But the magazine is aimed primarily at the average government employee, both because they are numerous and because they are in direct contact with the mass of the population at all times. They therefore constitute an easy-to-reach group of people who can act as field workers. They include teachers, nurses, midwives, technical health officers, social welfare officers, rural development officers and so on. *Famille et Développement* is a mine of information for their own training and information. It is of great value to them, because few scientific or other magazines are available, and those that are available are sold at prohibitive prices. In effect, then, *Famille et Développement* is the only magazine containing scientific information that is available to this group. Its articles are of good quality and are not difficult to understand.

In view of the modest salaries earned by its readers, the price of the magazine must remain low. For this reason *Famille et Développement* is being sold for 150 to 200 CFA francs, depending on the cost of living in the countries in which it is sold. This is four or five times lower than the cost of producing it.

Famille et Développement cannot be self-financing, since its purpose is the social welfare and education of its readers. From the outset it was decided that, unlike other international magazines, this could not be a commercial operation. If it were, it would lose over 80 percent of its intended audience. Just as no primary school, dispensary or social centre can provide its own financing, so *Famille et Développement* cannot exist without subsidies.

A multiplier effect is brought about through the direct contact government employees have with the wider public the magazine seeks to reach — a public it has been prevented from reaching because of language barriers. This audience includes those who do not speak French: the peasants, the artisans, and the vendors in the markets of our cities and countryside. Depending on the country, this represents between 40 and 60 percent of society.

No attempt at development that ignores this huge and largely illiterate majority will succeed. The working class is a yardstick by which to measure any process of social development, and on which social development must be focussed. Otherwise, development is no more than a façade. Until radio broadcasts can be made in African languages, the only way to reach the masses is to make use of government employees, who are in direct contact with these people.

If a revolutionary idea takes hold in the mind of the government employees, it will be transmitted to the masses. In the Third World such people are still the main medium through which to disseminate information. *Famille et Développement* is designed to take advantage of this fact. But it also contains information of interest to the rest of the world, since it is a good source of objective information on African problems and realities. Subscription to *Famille et Développement* will bring untold benefits to educational institutions, public libraries, training centres and even airline companies.

At present information travels from North to South, one-way. The Third World is a consumer of news. *Famille et Développement* will start a South-North current of information flowing from the developing world to the industrialized countries.

In generating information from the South, the magazine will bring to the developed half of mankind a wealth of information from the heart of African society; information that no amount of dedication, perspicacity or financial support on the part of international press agencies, special envoys or national correspondents can replace.

It will thus give the developed countries a better knowledge and appreciation of the Third World and will help to improve international understanding by removing many of the barriers that create prejudice among the world's peoples. By making use of this magazine, the developed countries can more effectively provide assistance to the Third World.

AN OBJECTIVE EVALUATION

When one has been involved in a project since its beginning, one cannot sing its praises without being suspected of partiality. For an objective appreciation of the magazine, let us consider the views of the readers themselves.

In the letters to the editor columns from the first issue on, spontaneous appraisals and suggestions have been made by government ministers, university professors, teachers, midwives, blacksmiths, students and others from Africa and elsewhere. People of all ages from all walks of life have voiced their opinions — and without exception they have been favourable.

The letters-to-the-editor columns of *Famille et Développement* are thus exceptional in the field of journalism in that they contain nothing but appreciative comments. Praise has come from every quarter: from Mali to Mauritius Island, from Zaire to the Federal Republic of Germany, Algeria and Switzerland. The compliments relate to the magazine's originality, its usefulness, its effect on the groups it seeks to reach, its helpfulness to government authorities, and its value to the developed countries.

From the first issue to the most recent, readers have been pleased with its originality:

There is a definite need for an original magazine like FD. It puts the emphasis back on the family rather than just the individual as a factor in development, on this continent in which the family has always had great significance. It opens the way for a psychosociological approach to economic phenomena. This cannot help but benefit all of Africa. . . Its scientific value will be indisputable if in the coming issues this variety of topics is dealt with. In this way the magazine might make a huge contribution toward demystifying subjects which have long been considered taboo on our vast continent.

> *(from the Director General of Instruction, Abidjan, Ivory Coast — 2nd issue)*

Your magazine deals with all aspects of Africa's problems, especially at the family level. We especially appreciate its objectivity and hope that your style will remain unchanged.

> *(from a group of young African and French sociologists in Paris — 13th issue)*

This is no ordinary magazine, but one that can be used as a manual to provide guidance.

FD is contributing energetically to the search for new bases for the economic, social and cultural development of the African continent. It not only raises problems; it also proposes solutions.

> *(from a reader in Bafoussam, Cameroon — 15th issue)*

Many readers have applauded the usefulness of *Famille et Développement*, which they feel provides them with a forum suited to their sociocultural environment and offers a wealth of information.

I was pleased and interested to receive from one of my pupils your first issue of November 1974. I cannot adequately express my appreciation for this magazine. There is a need in Africa today for more information in the field of education, especially among young people and women, who are the main participants in every form of social development.

I am in full agreement with the purposes and contents of this magazine, which should be a most useful instrument for educational institutions, and an effective means by which to develop and educate young African nations. . . It is "our" magazine. . .

> *(from a teacher in Bamako, Mali — 2nd issue)*

I greatly appreciated this magazine and its articles on current topics such as contraception and the grave issue of abortion.

I am a mother and I would like to receive every issue of this magazine (the first was loaned to me).

I do not subscribe to any magazine, since I have not found any which can command my full attention as this one does.

(from a mother in Lomé, Togo — 2nd issue)

FD is the type of magazine I have wanted to see for some time. It has come on the scene at a time when many of our values are being pushed aside in favour of others which will supposedly help promote development.

But despite the aid being provided by the rich countries, we are getting poorer all the time. We need to depend on nobody but ourselves.

FD has also raised problems which concern everybody, particularly families, namely abortion among students and family planning in this difficult life.

Other problems of concern these days are also dealt with in FD: one which concerns me is the direction in which the teaching profession is moving. . .

FD is within the reach of the person of average culture and is therefore of value to the majority of readers.

(from a teacher in Dakar, Senegal — 2nd issue)

Your first issue was a pleasant surprise. A news magazine such as this was needed in Africa and will no doubt experience considerable success.

We are students at the CM2 level in a village school. We have organized ourselves into working groups, and our group has discovered your interesting magazine. We want to surprise the whole class, and our teacher, the principal, has urged us to write you.

(from "Elephant" group, CM2 in Daloa, Ivory Coast — 6th issue)

FD is the type of magazine Africans have needed for 15 years. Its ideas and its outlook appeal to young people. Thank you for this African magazine which can help us solve our problems.

(from a pupil of GEG Bongouarou, Ivory Coast — 6th issue)

It is a pity that FD did not come out earlier. We might have avoided all the pitfalls which for many years elderly people of sixty and seventy like myself have had to cope with.

> *(from a blacksmith in Bamgassey par Toukotte, Mali — 9th issue)*

Many readers, especially young people and women, see *Famille et Développement* as being a valuable source of information, and wish to make a contribution:

> I wish to subscribe and also to offer a few ideas on the problems of young people, problems which are greatly disturbing to most of us. I have eight daughters and can therefore speak from personal experience.
> *(from a father in Dolisie, The Congo — 3rd issue)*

> I congratulate you. You cannot imagine how useful FD is to young people today.
> You have found the perfect formula. Your magazine is unique and it is an excellent source for training young people. As you know, some people are timid and do not wish to ask questions. Your magazine is helpful to them.
> I would like ten subscriptions for my pupils.
> *(from a priest at the St Michel College, Dakar, Senegal — 6th issue)*

> My interest in FD is mainly in its wide educational value for African intellectuals. It is also an instrument for education and for the exchange of ideas among all Africans.
> This magazine allows us to educate one another. It provides me with a means of assisting my brothers and sisters. . .
> *(from a government-employed midwife in Dakar, Senegal — 8th issue)*

> FD provides lucid, courageous and responsible coverage of prostitution and the problem of unwed mothers in Africa.
> To assist those wishing to help eliminate these two maladies, let us discuss them in FD and in some of the other magazines for African women.
> *(from a specialist in African wildlife in Savé, Bénin — 15th issue)*

Many readers of *Famille et Développement* point out that the magazine is well suited to their socio-cultural environment.

We are presently going through a sexuality crisis among our youth, in which the concepts imported from the West are being used, sometimes wrongly and sometimes correctly, and in which the vast amount of knowledge we have about traditional sex education is losing its value. I feel that this magazine is very timely, not only to inform us about sex-related problems but also to help us rediscover the abundant information we have on traditional sex education and to help us adapt to a society in which we are being turned about by every wind and doctrine coming from the West.

(from an African sociologist in Lomé, Togo — 3rd issue)

This educational development magazine has made me more aware of the reality of everyday life for most Africans regardless of their social milieu.

(from a reader in Porto-Novo, Bénin — 13th issue)

I feel that issues 5, 11 and 12 have been among the best. They contain items on juvenile delinquency, alcoholism and sexuality, all of which are devastating problems in our society.

(from a reader in Brazzaville, The Congo — 14th issue)

I enjoy reading your excellent magazine. . . I am writing to express my congratulations and my unqualified support for it. My reasons for doing so are simple: you are making a gigantic and truly admirable effort to denounce the obstacles to the development of Africa and you are constantly seeking to help your readers adapt to their surroundings.

(from a reader in Bamako, Mali — 14th issue)

Some readers have emphasized the contribution made by *Famille et Développement* toward improving the lives of people everywhere.

As a government nurse, I felt I knew everything about childbirth, but regular and attentive reading of FD has enabled me to learn more about my profession, and I realize that all my knowledge only amounts to a drop in the bucket.

(from a government nurse in Atitogon, Togo — 5th issue)

The health of mothers and children is a primary concern of Famille et Développement.

As a specialist in family planning and women's health care, I find in your articles proof that family planning is a concern throughout the world, especially in Africa.

(from a midwife in Oran, Algeria — 5th issue)

As an education magazine, FD should be of great assistance to teachers in helping them to achieve their goals. In addition, your magazine might gradually help both nurses and farmers to put new techniques into practice. . .!

(from a student in Piline, Senegal — 16th issue)

I have been a member of the Social Progress committee of my parish and a teacher-social assistant since 1965. Our committee organizes many training and education sessions on health and nutrition for rural social workers.

I must admit that my general perception of the problem of development and women's liberation has changed since I have been reading FD regularly. I understand more. . .

Its simple, clear style and illustrations make your magazine a teaching instrument that is indispensable to any social worker who wishes to learn more about helping people.

(from a teacher-social assistant at the Catholic Mission in Yangala, Zaire — 4th issue)

I am presently in charge of the development of rural agricultural assistance staff. Your magazine is one of the few if any that I know which provides motivation and updated knowledge on questions of development and education.

(from the Agricultural Training Centre in Gagnoa, Ivory Coast — 5th issue)

On this virtually illiterate continent, topics related to health or medicine should be presented using simple, practical examples. Studies should be carried out with a view to recommending uncomplicated health care methods.

Instead of doing this, we are spending huge amounts to subsidize the growing medical needs of the people by building hospitals, clinics or costly dispensaries. And in the meantime the masses are sinking deeper into poverty.

(from a technical health officer in Bafand, Cameroon — 13th issue)

Famille et Développement has received a favourable reaction from government authorities. In the Third World, where radio is an arm of the government, articles from the magazine are often broadcast in states such as Senegal, the Ivory Coast and Togo.

In Togo the *Famille et Développement* project has been "adopted" by the Ministry of National Education and Scientific Research. The educational reform that took place between 1970 and 1973 has introduced in the schools new disciplines such as national languages, home economics and sex education. In order that society, the family and the school may develop harmoniously, the reform document recommends that there be a continuing public information campaign on problems of sex education and family economy.

When *Famille et Développement* first came out, the Ministry of National Education and Scientific Research saw it as the most suitable instrument for this public information campaign and felt that it was a prerequisite for the success of the reform. The magazine is distributed in the school bookstores by the secondary school inspectors throughout the territory.

The underdeveloped countries are not the only ones who appreciate *Famille et Développement*. The magazine also has readers and admirers in the industrialized countries.

Congratulations on this extraordinary magazine with its fine photography and writing.

We are pleased with the selection and critical presentation and with the fact that these texts are being written by Africans. They truly demonstrate the complex reality of Africa instead of disseminating the views of a privileged few or propagating imported falsehoods. . .

FD helps us to maintain contact with Africa and its problems and to keep track of what is happening there, despite our distance from it.

(from a Swiss couple in Berne — 7th issue)

I wish to express my admiration and offer you my support. I find that FD, with its search for new avenues of development, is a fine alternative to a blind, slavish imitation of Europe. This is quite rare nowadays. . .

If I were an African I would work voluntarily for you. But I am European and I have a lot to do here. Nevertheless, I hope that we will remain in touch.

(from a teacher and editor of a university magazine in Kassel, Federal Republic of Germany — 16th issue)

In order to give more responsibility to the staff and to make *Famille et Développement* more a part of the African scene, in June 1978 the Association Africaine d'Education pour le Développement (ASAFED) was created and put in charge of the magazine by the IDRC, which continues to provide logistical support.

Convinced of the usefulness and effectiveness of *Famille et Développement*, other international agencies decided to assist the IDRC, which had provided the original support for the magazine. These included the UNFPA, the Ford Foundation, the Actions de Carême (Switzerland), the Coopération technique suisse, and the Swedish International Development Authority. The ASAFED hopes that African organizations and foundations will also contribute to this development education undertaking.

CHAPTER EIGHT

PROTEIN FROM PIG WASTE

LEE BOON YANG

Piggery wastes are a problem in Singapore, where large numbers of the animals are raised in a confined area. If the wastes could be treated and used for animal feed, a major source of pollution would be eliminated and substantial savings could be made in pig production. A project aimed at doing just this was approved by the IDRC in 1977 and has been funded in the amount of $302,985.

LEE BOON YANG is a graduate of the University of Queensland's school of veterinary science. He joined the primary production department of Singapore's Ministry of National Development in 1972, where his interest in animal waste utilization was aroused while studying the use of poultry litter in cattle feed. This led to his being assigned to head the IDRC-supported project described in this chapter.

THE NEED FOR SANITARY DISPOSAL and economic re-use of human and livestock wastes is of great importance in both developed and developing nations. Significant numbers of people are still living in conditions of poor environmental health and billions of dollars will be required to provide them with even basic sanitation. The UN General Assembly has recognized this and has proclaimed the 1980s the "International Drinking Water and Sanitation Decade."

In this era of environmental and resource consciousness, the concept of "wastes as resources" is widely appreciated. However the technology for putting this idea into effective use is not so widely practised because of various constraints and drawbacks. Scientists throughout the world have taken up this challenge and are concentrating enormous efforts on developing the means to control environmental degradation due to human activities effectively and economically. The Government of the Republic of Singapore and the International Development Research Centre are cooperating in such an effort.

ANIMAL WASTES IN SINGAPORE

The Republic of Singapore has a total land area of only 580 sq km. Although much of this land is being taken up by industrial, housing and water developments, there is a well-developed, intensive livestock industry producing sufficient pig and poultry products for domestic consumption. Scarcity of suitable agricultural land and the need to prevent pollution of the water catchment areas have resulted in further intensification of the livestock industry. The standing population of 0.8 million pigs and 12 million poultry produce almost 14 million litres of pig wastewater and 1,000 tonnes of poultry wastes per day. These wastes are a major source of organic pollution.

Conventional treatment of human or livestock wastewater often depends on mechanical aeration to stimulate bacterial growth for rapid breakdown of the wastes. These methods are well established in many parts of the world. However capital and operation costs are often very high, which severely limits their application to livestock wastes. Low-cost methods using anaerobic lagoons are available. Unfortunately such lagoons often give rise to obnoxious odours. Traditional methods of using the wastes as fertiliser by spreading it on the land cannot be practised in Singapore, owing to the absence of crop-land.

Hence there is a need to develop lower-cost alternatives to existing processes that will overcome the livestock wastes problem. Since Singapore imports all of its livestock feed, resource recovery from livestock wastes is particularly relevant.

With these considerations in mind, the Singapore Primary Production Department entered into a cooperative research venture with the IDRC. The project for "Pig Wastewater Purification, Reclamation and Algal Protein Recovery by High-Rate Pond System" (Algae Project in brief) was initiated in September 1977 with a grant of $272,000 from IDRC. This grant was to fund the first phase of the project which has the objective of establishing a high-rate pond system for purification of pig wastewater to permit water reclamation, minimum environmental pollution and maximum algal protein recovery and utilization as animal feed. A second phase study will also be undertaken to develop equipment and processes for harvesting micro-algae grown in high rate ponds. Arising from these research undertakings, a proper system of waste resource recovery will be developed to demonstrate its economic viability.

HIGH RATE PONDS FOR PROTEIN PRODUCTION

Algae are ubiquitous aquatic plants that range in size from single-celled microscopic forms (e.g. *Chlorella* and *Micractinium* spp.) to very large common seaweeds. They are capable of absorbing nutrients from the surrounding water and incorporating these by a light-controlled process called photosynthesis into new cell biomass. The value of such algae lies in the fact that algal cells contain 50 percent or more of protein. At the same time oxygen is released during photosynthesis, which supports bacterial degradation of the wastes to make them available as food for the algae.

High-rate algae ponds are adapted to utilise this natural process for treating wastewater which contains all the required nutrients for algae growth (Grisanti and Oswald, 1976). Such ponds are shallow to facilitate penetration of sunlight, and the contents are gently mixed to keep algal cells in suspension. Under such conditions the conversion of wastewater nutrients to algal protein occurs very rapidly and the attendant release of oxygen purifies the wastewater. Oswald (1963) described in detail the functioning of high-rate ponds for wastewater treatment.

McGarry (1971) studied high-rate ponds in Thailand using human wastes as substrate. Their results indicated that the productivity of high-rate ponds can be as high as 150 kg per ha per day, which is many times the protein productivity of conventional protein crops such as soybean. Shelef *et al* (1976) studied larger-scale high-rate ponds for municipal wastewater treatment and protein recovery. High organic loading rates in excess of 400 kg of BOD_5 per ha per day were found to be possible in Israel. Dugan et al (1972) in USA used poultry wastes successfully as a substrate for algae production in high-rate ponds. Dodd (1972) in USA, and Dodd and Anderson (1976) in Australia, researched the design and operation of high-rate ponds for treating municipal wastewater and the harvesting of algae for animal feed by a filtration method. The use of waste-grown algae as an animal feed was studied by Hintz *et al* (1966). Algae were found to be capable of supplying adequate protein and other essential elements to pigs, poultry and ruminant animals.

Although the potential of waste-grown micro-algae has been recognized for a long time (Burlew, 1953), harvesting is difficult because the algae are microscopic in size and present in low concentration in waste cultures. After 25 years of research, available algae harvesting techniques still have draw-backs that have hindered implementation of the concept. Centrifugation has been used to obtain uncontaminated algae for feeding experiments. Although effective, this method is too high in cost and required energy input to be practical. It appears that a more promising approach is to develop stable cultures of more filtrable algae, e.g. *Scenedesums, Micractinium* and *Oscillatoria.*

ALGAE PROJECT METHODOLOGY AND RESULTS

The IDRC recognized the need for research on a larger scale in the use of the high-rate pond concept for animal waste treatment and algal protein recovery. Hence in phase one of the Algae Project Singapore researchers have designed, constructed and are operating a series of high-rate ponds for treating pig wastewater in order to establish the conditions under which algae production can be optimized. At the time of writing, the project is operating 500 sq metres of pilot ponds and constructing another 2400 sq metres of demonstration ponds.

Stable cultures of *Micractinium* spp. have been maintained over the past 8 months of the operation. The algal biomass yield was found to be 170 kg per ha per day. Stability of the *Micractinium* culture is an important factor because it is a colonial alga suited for filtration removal. Although other researchers have seldom been able to achieve a nearly mono-species culture for an extended period on waste substrate in open ponds, our experience to date appears to indicate that this can be achieved under our conditions in Singapore.

Other project activities include the production of biogas from waste solids removed in the primary clarification of raw wastewater before loading into the ponds. This biogas will be used to provide energy for the postharvest processing of algae, thus enhancing the energy economy of the process. Current feeding experiments with steam-cooked, centrifuge-harvested algae fed to pigs has indicated that algal protein could replace a large proportion of soybean protein in the pig diet. In the first experiment conducted, algal protein replaced all soybean protein without significantly decreasing growth and carcass quality of pigs over a 3-month period.

During phase two, scheduled to begin in September 1979, the emphasis will be on development of innovative and economical algae harvesting systems. It is hoped the results will provide the break-through necessary for making the recovery of protein from pig waste or other organic wastes more than just a concept. It is an important step that could lead to practical application of this method of resource recovery to benefit mankind.

IMPACT OF THE ALGAE PROJECT

The project is still in its developmental stages; hence it is too early to categorize its total impact in absolute terms. However results now available indicate that large-scale culture of micro-algae on diluted pig wastewater is technically feasible, and promise to advance the state of the art to the point that it can be readily applied.

For Singapore, the most apparent benefit from such an application would be an effective and economical pig wastewater treatment system. This would provide a key to control the pollution of piggery waste. It would enable livestock farmers to continue their livelihood without encroaching on and destroying scarce water reserves, recreational areas and a generally healthy environment.

The application of the algae wastewater treatment system would also enable the reclamation of a large volume of water suitable for recycling as wash-water to farms. This would reduce farmers' need for costly potable water. In the drier season of the year, availability of recycled water would permit farmers to continue the good management practice of keeping pigs clean, thus minimizing the possibility of serious disease outbreaks.

Harvesting the algae cultured in high-rate ponds leads to recovery of biologically valuable protein suitable for use as animal feed. Production of algal protein will therefore contribute to the livestock economy in Singapore, which annually imports S$24 million of soybean products for animal feed.

Recovery of protein in this process also could have significant effects on the world food situation. Current livestock production practice in

Singapore and elsewhere is to use soybean products as the main source of protein for livestock feed. Therefore mass production of micro-algae and their substitution in animal feed would release large quantities of soybean for direct human consumption. This would make up for the protein deficit from which millions of people suffer in some regions of the world.

Application of algae technology is definitely not limited to Singapore. Given the climatic conditions of warm ambient temperature and ample sunshine, many tropical and subtropical countries are suitable for algae mass-culture. Provided that organic wastes are readily available, whether from livestock production units or human population, high-rate ponds can be used. The Singapore project will yield the required scientifically documented and evaluated results that will provide a sound basis for application and technology transfer to other countries.

In terms of technology transfer and expertise development, this project is staffed by Singapore scientists and engineers recruited from the ASEAN region. Only one part-time American consultant, with previous experience in algae technology, is employed on the project. This approach is much favoured by IDRC in order to develop local expertise. The "hands on" experience in operating and controlling the system through all phases of the project will set an example for the technical competence of most developing countries to cope with such novel wastewater treatment technology.

All the project facilities have been designed and constructed in Singapore using locally available manufactured items, equipment fabrication and construction skills. Only a minimum number of components such as pumps, centrifuge, specialized speed-reducing units, drum-dryer and instruments have been imported. The imported components have been of Asian manufacture in many cases, such as variable-speed motors and gearboxes used on the pond mixers for research purposes. This attempt to develop local technology has received IDRC's support and has resulted in project costs being far below that of comparable facilities in developed countries. It also put the Singapore model within the economic means of many developing countries. Thus in addition to providing the technology for waste treatment and resource recovery, mass-culture of micro-algae as developed in Singapore will also provide benefits to manufacturers and construction industries in countries that plan to adopt similar technology.

CONCLUSIONS

The Singapore project to recover protein from pig wastes is an example of adaptive technology transfer. Mass culture of micro-algae, though long recognized for its potential in sewage treatment, has not been studied as intensively for livestock waste treatment. Also, there are technological obstacles such as harvesting methods that need to be overcome before the process can be fully utilized. Singapore, with its intensive pig industry, was recognized by IDRC as having the unique potential to make an in-depth effort to apply known research findings to develop a new aspect of the concept, that of using pig wastes. The project is therefore playing a role in developing an appropriate technology for application in other countries.

REFERENCES

Burlew, J.S. (1953). Algal culture from laboratory to pilot-plant. Carnegie Institution of Washington. Publication No. 600. Washington D.C. USA.

Dodd, J.C. (1972). Harvesting of algae with a paper precoated belt-type filter. Ph.D. dissertation, University of California at Davis (1972).

Dodd, J.C., and J.L. Anderson (1976). An integrated high rate pond algae harvesting system. 8th Conference of the International Association on Water Pollution Research, Sydney, Oct. 1976.

Dugan, G.L., C.G. Golueke and W.J. Oswald (1972). Recycling system for poultry wastes. Journal of Water Pollution Control Federation. Vol 44. 432.

Grisanti, N.E. and Oswald, W.J. (1976). Protein from algae. Sessions on Processes for New Protein Food. American Institute of Chemical Engineers National Meeting. USA. 14 Apr. 1976.

Hintz, (1966) Ho F. et al (1966) Nutritive value of algae grown on sewage. J. of Animal Science, Vol 25 (3). 675 - 681.

McGarry, M.G. (1971) Unicellular protein production using domestic waste-water. Thai Journal of Agricultural Science. Thailand. Vol 4. 213-223.

Oswald, W.J. (1963) The high-rate pond in waste disposal. Developments in Industrial Microbiology, American Institute of Biological Sciences. USA.

Shelef, G., R. Morraine, A Meydan and E. Sandbank (1976). Combined algae production — wastewater treatment and reclamation systems. International Symposium on Microbial Conversion of Energy. Gottingen. Germany. Oct. 1976.

CHAPTER NINE

HELPING
YOUNG SCIENTISTS

GUILLERMO LOPEZ

Support for research in human reproduction is uneven among Latin American countries. On the whole, it is inadequate, and young scientists have few opportunities to enter the field. In 1974, the IDRC approved a grant of $330,000 to the Regional Population Centre in Bogota, Colombia, to help junior scientists obtain experience in clinical and experimental research in human reproduction and fertility regulation, through a program of awards. The Centre's grants have so far totalled $830,000.

GUILLERMO LOPEZ is president of the Corporación Centro Regional de Población, Bogotá, Colombia. A medical doctor, he took post-graduate training in reproductive biology. For some years he headed the gynecological department of Colombia's National Institute of Cancerology and was dean of clinical sciences at the National University. He has published more than 100 papers, mainly on obstetrics and gynecology, endocrinology, medical education, contraception and population.

SCIENCE AND TECHNOLOGY have recently emerged as important instruments in socio-economic development. As Chaparro[1] has pointed out, besides the purely scientific approach, which emphasizes only the development of a scientific infrastructure, and the economic approach, which deals exclusively with the "commercialization of technology", a third approach, based on a global vision of scientific and technological development, has recently been taking shape. This view does not limit itself indiscriminately to strengthening the national scientific and investigative capacity, nor does it confine itself to the problem of commercialization and adaptation of foreign technology.

This new perspective considers science and technology as two inseparable aspects of development, including not only the endogenous generation of scientific and technological knowledge, but the importation, adaptation and absorption of foreign technology as well. At the same time Koppelmanas[2] has pointed out that the advantage of having a number of separate contractual agreements (as opposed to a turnkey contract) is that such a system encourages the development of "national technological capabilities". Although some analysts of the developed world have expressed their belief[3] that on the basis of a strictly comparative observation of advantages, less-developed countries should not invest their scarce resources in scientific innovation and creation, and even though there is obviously no need for them to "re-invent the wheel", it is clearly essential for developing countries to benefit from their own participation in the world's scientific and technological development.

In a way, the case study we are about to examine — PLAMIRH (Latin American Program for Research in Human Reproduction) — embodies some of the above-mentioned concepts of the development and transfer of science and technology.

Knowledge in the biology of human reproduction has reached its present development thanks to the efforts of a number of researchers and institutions, among which the Latin American contribution must be recognized. The Ford Foundation, the World Health Organization's expanded program, the Population Council and the Rockefeller Foundation, among others, had previously contributed, through economic support, towards the development of research and training of personnel.

The study of reproduction in the subcontinent has suffered the same difficulties of any emerging new science and of any scientific and technological transfer. Despite the fact that research in this field is essential to Latin America, because of its patterns of reproductive growth, an inadequate infrastructure exists on the continent. There is not enough financial support; knowledge is uneven from institution to institution. In some areas there are scientists who carry out excellent research in the field, yet there are entire countries in which such enterprises are minimal. Trained and qualified young scientists do not have the necessary stimuli or support. Transfer of techniques is nearly impossible due to the lack of infrastructure, laboratory equipment or trained auxiliary personnel. In a quick scanning of the region, one could say that in some countries (Bolivia, Paraguay, Ecuador and Central American and Caribbean countries) research in reproductive biology is just beginning, while in others (Argentina, Chile, Uruguay, Brazil and Mexico) it is more developed. In still others, (Colombia, Peru, and Venezuela) research of good quality may be found, but it is limited to a few localized groups. In this regard the WHO Study Group on Strengthening of Resources in Developing Countries for Research in Human Reproduction[4] convened in Geneva in 1978, stated:

> In the context of general development in the less industrialized countries, the benefits of research on health problems are gaining increasing recognition. This had led to growing emphasis on self-reliance so that these countries may carry out such research, adapt technology, interpret advances made elsewhere and enable their scientists to make a full contribution to the solution, not only of local, but also of global problems.
>
> In the field of human reproduction and family planning, the large number of problems requiring research, their urgency and their complexity have stimulated the development of resources for research and have generated many professions of faith on the need to do more. However, little concrete guidance is available, in this field as in others, on how to strengthen research in developing countries.

THE PROGRAM

Seeking to improve that situation, a group of concerned Latin American scientists of different countries, decided — under the auspices of the IDRC and the Ford Foundation — to make a joint effort to develop a Latin American research program that would try to find a balance between experimental research in reproductive biology and research applied directly to the regulation of human fertility. The program was called PLAMIRH (Programa Latinoamericano de Investigaciones en Reproduccion Humana). Although it would be oriented to those aspects of reproductive biology related to human regulation, it would not be rigidly and exclusively limited to established themes, but would leave room for the development of spontaneous creativity on the part of researchers. Considering also that, although a number of researchers had been properly trained, this had not resulted in a substantial research output due to lack of economic support, the program would also appear as a basic means to correct this situation.

The safeguarding of the rights and welfare of those involved in research was given paramount importance in the program; any research would be carried out in accordance with national ethical or legislative codes, following the norms set forth by the Helsinki Declaration. There was an increasing awareness that good ethical review had to go hand-in-hand with severe and stringent technical review.

It is worthwhile to underscore that the decision made by the sponsoring agencies that the program should not only increase research potential but also be placed completely under the leadership and responsibility of the Latin American community, was a departure from previously established granting patterns.

This decision not only constituted a true challenge for scientists of the region, but also recognized that it is they who actually know the region's problems and its professional groups and their possibilities.

PLAMIRH has thus been a program directed, oriented, and executed by the Latin American scientific community. The board of directors consists of representatives of Latin American countries, chosen on their individual merit and rotated periodically. In planning, implementing and carrying out its studies, this board keeps constantly in mind the needs and cultural features of the region.

PLAMIRH's objectives have been spelled out as follows:

1. To promote and encourage new and creative ideas in the area of human fertility and its regulation by sponsoring research in the biology of reproduction, with emphasis on applied research.

2. To grant priority to qualified young researchers, although the program is opened to all Latin American researchers.

3. To encourage a larger number of researchers to enter the field of reproductive biology and to increase their productivity.

The clinical and experimental research to be promoted and financed was limited to the following areas: neuroendocrinology; hypophyseal function; gonads (oogenesis, follicular maturation, corpus luteum inhibition and stimulation of ovulation, gametogenic and endocrine testicular function); male and female genital tract; fertilization, implantation and nidation; lactation; epidemiological and clinical trials on aspects related to human reproduction in the region; and studies on primates and other animals from the region as experimental models.

The hypophyseal aspects of pregnancy and delivery, placental endocrinology and human genetics studies of immediate clinical application were also included later in the program's operation. The main reason for restricting the studies so specifically was the underdevelopment of the listed research areas compared to others, which already had been the subject of more advanced studies in Latin America.

In order to establish mechanisms with which to evaluate research proposals, PLAMIRH has obtained the collaboration of 53 highly qualified Latin American researchers located in various countries of the region. These constitute the Scientific Committee. Each project is analyzed by three separate members of this committee, to whom the project is sent according to their own particular field of specialization.

An Executive Secretariat for the program was established in a non-profit private research and training institution in Colombia: the CCRP (Corporacion Centro Regional de Poblacion, Carrera 6 No. 76-34, Bogotá, Colombia, South America), which provides the physical and administrative facilities for the operation of the program.

RESULTS

Through four years of the program's operation to November 30, 1978, PLAMIRH has received 240 proposals requesting support for research on reproductive biology. After routine evaluation, 129 have been approved and funded. Besides these, 32 renewals have been awarded to projects that after a year's work obtained results that justified their continuation. The total amount disbursed directly to researchers in their respective countries is US$999,464. This figure represents 77 percent of PLAMIRH's total budget; the rest includes expenses for meetings of the Board of Directors, evaluation expenses, salaries, mailing costs, communications, copies, etc. Therefore, considering the geographical area covered and the wide scope of the program, administrative costs have been kept at a surprisingly low level.

Although the quality of the research promoted cannot be measured exclusively by the number of publications or presentations made, publication in journals of good standing or presentation at high-level conferences are indicators of quality accepted by the world's scientific community. During PLAMIRH's four years there have been a total of 154 publications in different journals and PLAMIRH researchers have made 121 presentations at national and international meetings. The number of presentations and papers published is rising. A good example is provided by the last meeting of ALIRH (one of the most prestigious Latin American scientific societies concerned with reproduction), which was held in Cali on March 6-9, 1977: half of the four-day program consisted of papers on PLAMIRH-sponsored research awards.

One of PLAMIRH's main objectives is to help young researchers. Youthfulness is, of course, a relative concept, particularly among research professionals in the biology of reproduction, who at present must undergo long training periods. Nevertheless, more than half of PLAMIRH's grants have been given to individuals under 40 years of age. At least 73 young researchers working on projects awarded by PLAMIRH have been won over to reproduction research and have received in-service training. Furthermore, research work sponsored by PLAMIRH has been the source of more than 28 Master's or Ph.D. theses and monographs.

Those directing the program have tried to keep a balance between basic and applied research, while realizing that these are also relative terms and that there is a strong debate among scientists and administrators as to what constitutes an appropriate balance. It is well known that groups dedicated to basic research often have had to request the assistance of clinical researchers in order to complete and broaden their work, and vice-versa. Competent clinical and laboratory researchers have to rely on each other.

The geographical distribution of research proposals, grants and renewals by countries is given in Table 1.

Table 1
DISTRIBUTION OF REQUEST PROPOSALS, RENEWALS
& GRANTS GIVEN BY COUNTRIES

Countries	Requests	Grants	Renewals	Total Granted
Argentina	98	51	17	68
Bolivia	2	—	—	—
Brazil	24	7	1	8
Colombia	13	8	2	10
Chile	41	24	5	29
Ecuador	3	—	—	—
Mexico	18	14	3	17
Paraguay	2	2	—	2

Perú	16	14	1	15
Dominic Rep.	1	1	—	1
Uruguay	15	7	3	10
Venezuela	2	1	—	1
Total	235	129	32	161

COMMENTS

PLAMIRH has definitely been a useful project. It has not only ful-filled its objectives — promoting research in the biology of reproduction, helping young researchers establish themselves, encouraging scientists to work in bio-reproduction and keeping them recognized. It has gone beyond, becoming the cornerstone upon which this type of research rests in Latin America, particularly now when most other sources have been diminishing or disappearing. In some cases, PLAMIRH-sponsored projects have pre-vented the disbanding and emigration of groups of researchers who were struggling to live through the political difficulties of the moment.

The figures previously quoted measure, to some extent, the impact of the program on the scientific community, improving the capacity of indi-genous scientists to do research in what they feel are the important problems in the field. Nevertheless, there is still room for improvement. A surge in em-phasis on the andrological aspects of reproduction has arisen spontaneously from the scientists (22 percent of grants given). Projects have been approved concerning conditions peculiar to the region, e.g., high-altitude reproductive aspects; folkloric plants used for contraception; the reproductive pattern in captivity of *Desmodus Rotundus*, a local bat species; hypothalamic-hypophyseal functioning in schistosomiatic patients in Brazil. But perhaps an approach epidemiologically oriented to Latin American conditions, or the strengthening of more applied or applicable research could be reinforced. PLAMIRH's directors are aware of such needs and steps have been taken to this end.

The geographical concentration of research projects in certain re-gions has been another matter of concern for the program's directors. The problem here is a different one. It is quite logical that laboratories with a long tradition in research are apt to present the best proposals, and these, of course, will have better chances of being approved. During PLAMIRH's first year of existence, a few institutional grant applications were drawn up in an attempt to develop new research institutes, but none was put forward. It is now clear to the directors that in order to create a research capacity from scratch — that is, to develop new research, and different mechanisms — a larger infrastructure and much greater financial support are needed, which

are beyond the program's capacity under the present conditions. It is de-
cidedly not enough to help one or two researchers, or to acquire a few pieces
of laboratory equipment, technical assistance, and sporadic supervision.
Long-term basic and short-term practical training programs must be established, as well as adequate conditions for researchers and auxiliary personnel. In other words, a "critical mass" has to emerge, which includes not only
scientists, local physical facilities, auxiliary personnel and equipment, but
most important of all, the proper surroundings. This will lead to a build-up
of multidisciplinary groups that could achieve greater output than individual
scientists working in isolation.

To quote again the WHO Study Group already mentioned: "Stable
core support for a number of years is considered to be a prerequisite for
launching of research groups and will probably have to continue to come
largely from other than national sources". . . . From the case histories studied,
it was, moreover, quite evident that the substantial external support will
continue to be needed after a 10-year period. This may require a radical
change in the thinking of agencies promoting and supporting the strengthening of developing countries' resources for research in human reproduction".

PLAMIRH has been very well received by the scientific community
in Latin America. The occasional criticism that it excludes some aspects of reproduction because they already had support, or that the criteria for scientific evaluation sometimes appeared too strict, have been appeased through
time and performance. Notwithstanding this acceptance and the successful
impact on scientists, the program needs more time and diffusion to reach
governmental policy- and decision-makers. Very positive reactions have
been received from the public sector in some countries — Colciencias in Colombia, the Academy of Sciences in Argentina, the Scientific Council of Brazil and others. But still more has to be done so that governments will look at
PLAMIRH as an entity offering valuable assistance and consultancy for their
local research needs.

This assessment of PLAMIRH would necessarily be incomplete unless another very valuable asset were brought out — what might be called the
IDRC contribution to international development: the criteria and approach
with which IDRC and the Ford Foundation, the original donor agencies,
agreed to set up the enterprise. Giving "free and open stance" to a group of
Latin American scientists for the guidance and implementation of the program from the start, is a most important departure from the usual paternalis-
tic granting patterns seen in this type of undertaking. In spite of the existence
of patent agreements, the orientation and decisions, the ups and downs of
the program have been borne by the Latin American groups. PLAMIRH has
been a program *originated by* Latin American scientists, *developed by* Latin
Americans and *for* Latin Americans in a Latin American socio-cultural
environment.

On the basis of this experience, those involved in the transfer of
science and technology from developed to developing nations could gain

profitable insights that could assist them in the orientation and improvement of technical cooperation and cooperative programs as positive contributing factors for a better developing world.

REFERENCES

1. F. Chaparro. La Planificación del desarrollo científico-tecnológico. Aspectos que cubre y estrategias de acción. Memorias del Seminario sobre tecnología industrial. Instituto de Investigaciones Tecnológicas. Bogotá. Feb. 1975.

2. Lazare Koppelmanas, UNIDO, ID/WD,64/11.970 quoted by C. Cooper and F. Sarcovitch. The Mechanism for Transfer of Technology from Advanced to Developing Countries UNCTAD Intergovernmental Group on Transfer of Technology mimeo November 1970.

3. R.S. Eckans. Notes on Incentives and Innovation in Less Developed Countries. American Economic Review Papers and Proceedings May 1966. As quoted by J. Katz and R. Cibotti. Marco de Referencia para un programa de investigaciones en temas de ciencia y tecnología en América Latina. BID/CEPAL/BA/10/NN1976.

4. WHO Research in Human Reproduction: Strengthening of Resources in Developing Countries. Report of WHO Study Group. World Health Organization. Technical Report Series. 627. W.H.O. Geneva, 1978.

CHAPTER TEN

DEFENCE AGAINST FAMINE

BRHANE GEBREKIDAN

Ethiopia is believed to be the home of sorghum, a staple food crop not only for Ethiopians but for hundreds of millions who live in the semi-arid tropics. When sorghum crops fail, famine follows in Ethiopia. Addis Ababa University's agricultural faculty has for many years been carrying out research aimed at improving sorghum, and in 1972 the IDRC granted it $195,300 to continue this work. In 1974 a further $560,000 grant was approved.

BRHANE GEBREKIDAN, leader of the project he describes in this chapter, is an Ethiopian whose degrees are in plant sciences (Addis Ababa), agronomy (Nebraska) and plant breeding (Minnesota). He has done research in both maize and sorghum and is National Task Force Leader for the Improvement of Ethiopian Field Food Crops and editor of the *Ethiopian Journal of Agricultural Sciences*. He has been the national coordinator of sorghum improvement in Ethiopia since 1969.

THE LIVES AND WELL-BEING of millions of rural Ethiopians traditionally have been intertwined with the status of the sorghum crop. A
year of good sorghum harvest is often a year of prosperity, but if
the sorghum crop fails, food supply is scarce and famines become common-
place.

Ethiopia, in fact, is probably the original home of sorghum and is
the source of many wild and cultivated forms adapted to a wide range of
growing conditions. Consequently Ethiopia is a valuable reservoir of diverse
genetic material for sorghum breeders throughout the world.

Sorghum is the dominant crop in parts of the country where
drought and moisture shortage are the norm. In most of these areas, the traditional sorghums, though requiring a long growing season, give reasonable
harvests in years of good rainfall. But they fail to produce any grain if the
rains are inadequate. The recent droughts that have dominated these zones,
along with most of Sahelian Africa, have caused the failure of the sorghum
crop and resulted in massive famines and deaths. These painful experiences
have forced the rural people in these areas to look for ways of stabilizing
crop production. Realizing such a need, the Ethiopian Sorghum Improvement Project (ESIP) was created with financial support from the IDRC. It has
tried to introduce early-maturing varieties along with recommended production packages. This has been done by holding field days near the project
sites, carrying out demonstrations in selected farmer's fields, and through the
Extension and Project Implementation Department (EPID), the Settlement
Authority, and State Farms. Farmers in such areas are now becoming more
aware of the potential of early-maturing and drought-avoiding sorghums
adapted to the environment, pest and disease situation of the area. The demand for such sorghums is increasing in these areas.

However, a positive influence on food production depends on a
multi-disciplinary approach. And since the ESIP has not been in operation

long enough to coordinate all disciplines and agencies influencing sorghum production in Ethiopia, and because varietal development is long-term by its very nature, the project's direct influence on sorghum production in Ethiopia has so far been modest. Even this modest influence cannot be quantified because of the absence of reliable crop production statistics. For similar reasons, it is difficult to predict the future impact of ESIP on Ethiopian sorghum production. However, the outstandingly successful breeding program that has been established shows promise of making a major contribution to the country's food supplies. The project's main contribution to food production has been supplying improved varieties and recommending optimum packages of production including seeds, fertilizers and cultural practices. The varieties that have been developed or introduced by the project and are being grown in different parts of the country in varying amounts are Gambella 1107, Dedessa 1057, Kobomash 76, Serena, Alemaya 70, and Awash 1050.

Two of these high-yielding cultivars, Alemaya 70 and Awash 1050, substantially outyield farmers' cultivars in high and intermediate altitude zones respectively. In the low rainfall areas these new varieties can give up to approximately 5.0 tons/ha and in the high rainfall areas they produce up to 8.0 tons/ha on small experimental plots. Average on-farm yield of the farmers' cultivars is about 1 ton/ha.

For lowland areas, suitable maturing varieties are almost absent. Kobomash 76 has been released due to a crisis situation resulting from the drought: it has performed well in other parts of the world but has not been tested extensively under Ethiopian conditions. In 1976 it has yielded 3.5 tons/ha under experimental conditions.

A number of trials have been carried out to define packages of agronomic packages for growing the new sorghum cultivars in the various regions of the country.

An important part of the research program has been to determine the major diseases and pests of sorghum in Ethiopia along with the most commonly found weeds, and to develop methods for their control. Surveys have shown that weed control is important since competition from weeds can reduce yields by at least 25 percent. Tests conducted on the major broadleaf weeds indicate that atrazine-based herbicides are the most effective form of control. A major unsolved problem is the development of a control for the parasite witchweed, striga. It is believed that if the weed can be effectively controlled, a major hurdle will be overcome in increasing Ethiopian sorghum output. A limited striga control program is currently being undertaken in the project.

The surveys have also identified 12 major sorghum diseases and 13 types of pests, which have been classified into general, highland or lowland specific, and/or high rainfall-low rainfall specific. This classification allows researchers to estimate the frequency of occurrence of the various pests and diseases by region, and to concentrate their control efforts in those areas.

One of the objectives of ESIP has been the collection of Ethiopian sorghums. As of the 1977 crop season there was a collection of Ethiopian sorghum varieties numbering over 5,700. This collection has been made freely available to other cooperating national programs and to ICRISAT. The varietal development program has concentrated on pure line selection, the pedigree method and hybridization.

For pure line selection, ESIP has been gathering between 500 to 1,000 new Ethiopian sorghums every year and growing them out for evaluation purposes. The pedigree method is the crossing program involving Ethiopian and exotic varieties. In total there are 137 parents involved in 11 major combination blocks. A hybrid program started in 1977, and is based on 10 male sterile lines and 163 pollinators. Combinations were made in the off season nursery and 1,630 different F_1 hybrids were planted for yield trials in 1977.

GOVERNMENT AND NATIONAL DEVELOPMENT POLICIES

ESIP has become an excellent example of effective cooperation between the Addis Ababa University (AAU) and the Institute of Agricultural Research (IAR). The two institutions, along with IDRC, have different vital contributions that make the effective functioning of ESIP possible.

AAU and IAR have agreed to give all national responsibility for improvement of the sorghum crop to ESIP. Almost all research stations and other government organizations interested in sorghum receive seeds, guidance, and consultancy from the project. The project has now become the national reference centre for almost all aspects of Ethiopian sorghum improvement and production. Though ESIP attends to such references with pleasure, we find that this unlimited role is demanding increasingly more time of our very limited professional staff.

In the National Crop Improvement Committee (NCIC) framework, ESIP is the coordinator for all national sorghum trials and nurseries. This responsibility entails organizing and planning trials, packaging and distributing seeds, providing instructions and data sheets for the trials, providing consultancy and advice on sorghum, assembling data from all cooperators, analyzing and interpreting the data, and submitting reports on work done on the crop during the year to the NCIC annual meetings. In addition to these functions, ESIP is nationally responsible for breeding, germ plasm collection and introduction, and agronomic and crop protection trials on sorghum. ESIP often calls ad hoc technical meetings of cooperators and appropriate crop protection and soils specialists to review the national work on sorghum. Visits by these experts to various stations handling sorghum trials are also arranged by ESIP. The project is considered significant in the NCIC framework not only as an effective crop-specific project but also as a model that appears

Searching for a better grain in Ethiopia, the home of sorghum.

to positively influence modes of operation and crop improvement approaches in the other nationally important field crops.

The Ethiopian Seed Corporation (ESC), which has been recently established, depends entirely on ESIP as a source of breeder and foundation sorghum seed for all ecological zones of the country. ESIP played a prominent catalytic role in the establishment of the ESC, and sorghum is one of the top priority crops for seed production by ESC.

Another important agency with a strong interest in the activities of ESIP is the Ethiopian government's Relief and Rehabilitation Commission (RRC). Since the RRC's chief geographical areas of activity are major sorghum producing zones, the crop is often of highest priority for the commission. The commission is very keen to popularize ESIP's new sorghum culti-vars, which can stabilize crop production in the drought- and famine-prone areas of the country. In one such difficult crop production area, Kobo, the seed multiplication farm of the Kobo-Alamata Regional Agricultural Development Project of the RRC, is entirely dependent on ESIP as a source of breeder and foundation seed, as well as technical information on sorghum seed production.

Realizing the menace of *quelea* birds (also known as weaverbirds) to sorghum production, the Ministry of Agriculture and Settlement has recently established a Quelea Control Project. The activities of this project and that of ESIP have become mutually supportive. Indirectly, ESIP played a catalytic role in the establishment of the Quelea Project.

ESIP plays significant roles in the government's policy formulations not only in sorghum research but also in production. On the production side, we find ESIP's linkages are directly with State Farms, the Settlement Authority, and the various Regional Agricultural Development Units. To each of these, ESIP provides technical consultancy and advice, seed and production recommendations.

In general, ESIP's impact on government and national development policies, particularly as related to sorghum, is multifaceted: sometimes it assumes a catalytic role, at other times it gets involved in policy formulations, and sometimes it acts as consultant and advisor. Whatever the role may be in national sorghum research, extension, production, and development policies, ESIP is a unit that is seldom ignored.

THE SCIENTIFIC COMMUNITY

The impact of ESIP on the Ethiopian scientific community is significant: it is often a major participant in professional dialogues. And the comprehensive sorghum improvement activity of the project is often referred to as a model crop improvement program by the scientific community, which indicates its high regard for it.

ESIP continues to play a major catalytic role in encouraging and stimulating other Ethiopian scientists to be more involved in sorghum-related investigations such as pathology, entomology, nutrition, quelea and striga control. ESIP is also the major force cultivating team spirit among Ethiopian workers interested in sorghum.

ESIP is an active member of both the Ethiopian Seed Corporation Technical Advisory Committee and Ethiopian Plant Genetic Resources Centre Advisory Council. In both, the project's services and contributions are vital, and its positive influences in such groups are well appreciated by the scientific community. The project, in fact, played an active role in establishing both these important organizations. Significant contributions continue to be made by ESIP to both, not only in ideas but through its collections of invaluable germ plasm. As mentioned earlier, all basic and foundation seeds of improved sorghum cultivars are provided by ESIP to the ESC. ESIP has contributed a total of 5,000 accessions of Ethiopian sorghum germ plasm to the Ethiopian Genetic Resources Centre. Scientific interactions on these and related items in which ESIP is a leading participant, go on continuously.

ESIP also adds continuously to the scientific knowledge of Ethiopian sorghums through the literature. The ESIP annual reports are important references in most national agricultural experiment stations and educational institutions. Our annual workshops and field days serve as important scientific forums of interaction on Ethiopian sorghum improvement. The regular annual NCIC reports provide us with a good opportunity to address the whole sector of the Ethiopian scientific community that focuses on crops. The results of these interactions often give us new insights into Ethiopia's sorghum improvement efforts. In addition, ESIP reaches the scientific community on specific topics in national, regional, and international scientific publications. On the whole, ESIP's contributions and presence are well felt by the Ethiopian scientific community.

OTHER CONTRIBUTIONS

One way in which ESIP has had a considerable impact on the Ethiopian scene is by developing a high quality, viable and comprehensive sorghum improvement program using entirely local staff. The program has now matured enough for it to pay attention to most of the needs of the major sorghum ecological zones of the country. This strength and development has come about mainly because of ESIP's emphasis on training local staff. Within ESIP, we now have an adequate supply of fully-trained technical assistants who can carry out almost all skilled jobs related to sorghum improvement in both field and laboratory. Our training efforts have been useful also to other national organizations such as the Ethiopian Seed Corporation, the National Development Campaign, EPID and the Regional Agricultural Development Projects. ESIP staff have major roles in the teaching and curriculum development activities of the Ethiopian Colleges of Agriculture. ESIP's strong, comprehensive sorghum improvement program and the well-developed Ethiopian network of sorghum stations have been among the major reasons for the establishment of a graduate studies program in plant sciences in this country. ESIP's total contribution to the country's trained agricultural manpower, at both high and intermediate levels, has been significant.

ESIP is now considered a very important unit in a worldwide network of sorghum improvement centres. Ethiopian sorghum germ plasm, collected, evaluated, and distributed by ESIP, is considered invaluable and is well known in most international, regional, and national sorghum improvement programs.

NON-TECHNICAL PROBLEMS

There have been two general types of problems encountered by ESIP — technical and non-technical. The technical problems have been dealt with in ESIP's Progress Report No. 5, 1977. I will deal with the main non-technical problems.

The lack of a seed production establishment of any sort in the country has been the main factor limiting the spread of improved varieties to farmers. The recent establishment of the Ethiopian Seed Corporation is expected to alleviate this problem. Sorghum is one of the priority crops for the Corporation and ESIP is supplying the breeder and foundation seeds.

Another important problem has been — and continues to be — the lack of effective linkage between the crop improvement program and the national extension service. ESIP continues to feel that it must have a strong outreach program as an integral part of its activities.

The third important problem is the impossibility or difficulty of obtaining suitable research equipment and supplies from local or foreign sources through local agents. This problem often exists even if money for the purchase of this material is available.

ADVANTAGES AND DIFFICULTIES OF COOPERATION WITH IDRC

ESIP's feelings about the advantages and difficulties associated with cooperating with IDRC have been honestly expressed in our Project Annual Reports.

We consider the disadvantages of cooperation with IDRC on the whole to be minor. However, for the sake of completeness and looking at the issue from all angles, one point will be mentioned here.

Even though we fully appreciate the importance of periodic technical and financial reports, the centre's requirement that these reports be submitted on a specific date sometimes makes it very difficult to submit technical reports that are meaningful. Our technical reports naturally depend on the data we collect from a given growing season. Often, we are asked to submit a technical report even before harvests have been completed.

The major aspect we continue to appreciate and admire is the IDRC's total belief and confidence in a project that is completely staffed by local personnel. This is unlike most aid-giving foreign agencies, which invariably attach strings and insist that their own nationals must be posted to projects they are financing.

The minimum of bureaucracy involved in our dealings with the IDRC makes our project operations efficient and less time-consuming. The prompt and efficient responses to ESIP enquiries from IDRC offices is another quality of the Centre we value highly.

ESIP's semi-autonomous status, which has been made possible by the mutual agreement between IDRC, AAU, and IAR, has been one of the most favourable reasons for the project's smooth and efficient operations. We cannot overemphasize the importance of adequate financial support for the effective operation of a project such as ESIP. We feel that one of the most important advantages of cooperating with IDRC has been the good financial support we have received from the Centre.

Inasmuch as we are located in an area where current scientific literature on sorghum virtually does not exist, the services of the IDRC library in providing ESIP with regular computer printouts of published topics on sorghum, and the associated photocopy supply of selected papers are invaluable to our project. Thanks to this service we are kept up-to-date on scientific developments on sorghum even though we have no library of any sort within everyday reach. This service keeps our scientific morale constantly high and makes us feel we are not left out and are communicating with the world-wide scientific community that works with sorghum.

The periodic personal visits of IDRC staff and the sincere interest of the Centre in the project are much appreciated by ESIP. Such visits give us constant encouragement to strive to do better and contribute a great deal to strengthening the ties between the Centre and this project.

CHAPTER ELEVEN

A MODEL OF RURAL DEVELOPMENT

Planners once thought that to improve the lives of rural families it was enough to provide them with knowledge about new food production technologies. That view was discarded when rural development did not automatically follow from agricultural extension efforts. A project developed in the Eastern Cundinamarca district of Colombia took into account, in addition to technological factors, both economic and social ones in trying to improve local farmers' standard of living. The project, begun in 1971, received a total of $910,000 in IDRC grants.

This report has been approved by JOSUÉ FRANCO (photo), general manager of the Instituto Colombiano Agropecuario (ICA), and Jaime Isaza, vice-manager for rural development. The text was prepared by Agustín Cobos, director of information and programming of ICA's technical assistance division, and Nestor Castro, director of the Cáqueza district, ICA's Region 1.

THE FIRST EFFORTS to disseminate new agricultural technology in Colombia were based on community development and agricultural extension programs. In 1970 measures were taken to introduce the results of the green revolution: the use of improved seeds, fertilizers and agronomic practices to make the agricultural and cattle-raising activity of the small farmer more productive.[8]

At that time the small farmer was generally believed to be inefficient in the use of the existing resources. Those who believed this forgot that the type of programs being promoted did not always suit local conditions, and that the new technology by itself was not enough to ensure its adoption and to raise the farmer's standard of living, or to produce a meaningful increase in the national economic growth.

Technological changes demanded greater inputs: for low-income farmers this often meant contracting debts they could not absorb. It was then necessary to include institutional changes in areas such as credit and marketing, new production technologies, new types of institutions and organization, and better use of existing local resources. Otherwise, as in fact was then the case, the beneficiaries of technological change would continue to be the producers who hold greatest control over the production factors (land, capital, work).[15]

In 1968, in view of the minor impact the extension programs made, the agricultural and cattle raising sectors were restructured in Colombia. The Instituto Colombiano Agropecuario (ICA) ceased to be an institution dedicated exclusively to research and became a *research and extension* institute. The methodology used for serving the small farmer was based on spreading the new technology generated by the experimental stations through farm visits and demonstrations as the only activity required for technological development. However, the adoption rates were still low.

Gradually, through field experience, the sociological factors that limited the adoption of new technology on the part of small farmers became apparent: low levels of education, health, nutrition and community organization. These, together with the problems of land and capital (credit), helped to orientate action towards the new concept of *rural development*[8].

RURAL DEVELOPMENT

After the study carried out by Colombian experts on rural development projects in other countries, it was concluded that the model of the Puebla Project, in Mexico, was the most suitable. However, this project had limited its activities to corn, and ICA did not want to overlook the fact that in most smallholding areas in Colombia multiple cropping is used as an answer to the constraints imposed by the size and quality of the holding and seasonal rainfall. ICA intended to emphasize both social welfare and production.

ICA therefore defined its goals for the rural development program of the country as follows: "To generate, test and develop strategies to confront the problems limiting social and economic development in specific geographic areas characterized by small farmers producing at the subsistence level, through the incorporation of technologies to adequately increase in the region the production of basic and traditional goods in order to improve nutrition and income"[9].

To implement this concept, in 1970 ICA chose some suitable areas of action. At the end of 1971 the first four *rural development projects* replaced the old *extension agencies*. These projects worked on several fronts through schemes that made better use of the professional staff. The projects combined the transfer of agricultural technology with a credit orientation process for vegetable and animal species, home industries, home improvement, family kitchen gardens, etc. The diagnostic studies of the rural communities defined rural development as a concept implying a coordinated action of the government in the following areas: credit, transfer of technology, trading and marketing, provision of services, infrastructure and social welfare. One of those projects was the Rural Development Project of Eastern Cundinamarca, known as the Cáqueza Project, in which the International Development Research Centre participated at ICA's request.

THE PROJECT

The project started activities in the premises of a previous extension agency. Most of the initial efforts were devoted to carrying out the agronomic trials in which the agency had engaged through an ICA-FAO agreement. Simultaneously, PDROC started another series of trials, which were conceptually different from the first one and reflected the influence of the Puebla

Plan in Mexico[6]. There were certain differences between the two types of experiments. The ICA-FAO experiments were planned at national level; they usually studied the behavior of two agronomic variables (genotypes and fertilization) and were more an attempt to demonstrate the recommendation generated by the Experimental Centre. In contrast, the project trials were planned at local level and searched for answers to specific problems of variables such as genotypes, fertilization levels, sowing distance, planting dates and weed control. The basic objective was to generate technological packages better adapted to the biophysical conditions of the region, and more easily acceptable to the small farmer.

Thus although the project goals included a global understanding of the production system of the small farmer, the initial work placed more emphasis on production aspects. However, towards the end of 1971 it was possible to identify the emergence of an enlarged concept of development that would make it possible to take socio-economic aspects into consideration, permitting analysis of the different factors affecting the rural family's welfare[6].

The old rural extension model (which considered the dissemination of new technology generated by the experimental stations as the only activity required for the technological development of small farmers) was gradually forgotten. It was replaced by the idea that it was necessary to have a better knowledge of local production systems before attempting to change them. In this, the project followed the philosophy — and key to success — of the Borgo a Mozzano Project in Italy, which proclaimed the need for an intimate knowledge of the region, its people and problems before attempting to improve the situation.

Many of the project's relevant experiences have been based on an interpretation of the region in terms of its agricultural-biophysical, infrastructural, demographic and institutional characteristics, obtained through socio-economic studies.

As a result, the project team accepted the need and value of the socio-economic research studies and recognized that their final objective was not merely to increase production per unit in the area. The need to have a model for rural development became gradually clearer.

The model developed in cooperation with the project team focussed on the identification of the mechanisms that intervene in rural development and the search for sources of reference in relation to methodology for development. For convenience sake the model was completely hypothetical but it was designed to provide the necessary flexibility for change[7].

Although there can be a wide range of models, depending on the specific interests and training of those who design it, the Cáqueza Project consciously attempted to include both economic and social variables in order to make use of the experiences and ideas of the project's personnel and to include the priority variables indicated by the diagnostic study.

IMPACT OF THE PROJECT

The project has had repercussions within ICA. For the purpose of this review, they are divided into those that affected the different teams and beneficiaries of the project at both local and national levels and those that affected the institution and the staff responsible for designing rural development methodologies according to the policies outlined by the government.

ON LOCAL GROUPS

The existence of a rural extension program that had little impact on traditional agriculture together with an awareness of the progress being made by other developing countries through the Green Revolution, persuaded the farmers and technicians of different projects in Colombia (particularly Cáqueza) to adopt a new working system, although its results were still difficult to foresee at the time. As we will see later, the benefits of this new approach may well have been greater for the experts than for the farmers involved. However, it is to be expected that the work now being carried out with groups of small farmers will reverse this distribution of benefits.

ON PROJECT EXPERTS

The experience acquired by the project teams, particularly during the first year, led to greater understanding and new ideas about rural development.

The interaction of the team and the farmers showed the team that, before attempting any change, it was necessary to observe and describe precisely the biophysical environment as well as the production systems and the farmer's constraints[12].

The design and adoption of the model helped them to truly understand their role and position, as well as the assignment of priorities and the elaboration of more precise action programs. Gradually, as these programs were implemented, the process of non-formal training for the project team kept growing, so that at the end of the fifth year their concepts of rural development greatly differed from those they had at the beginning. They also differed from those of technicians working in projects where such strategies had not been tried.

At present, most of these experts hold key positions within the structure of ICA's rural development program, both at regional and national level, and their experience and knowledge are constantly shared through training courses.

ON FARMERS

One of the concrete results of the project was to provide the basis of evaluating its impact over a period of time, both qualitatively and quantitatively. At present, however, it is only possible to describe that impact qualitatively in terms of the following aspects:

— The motivation and training provided by the project's personnel for the organization of farmers in groups, which made possible a considerable increase in the farmers' ability to request institutional services.

— The construction of eight shovel and pike roads, through the coordination of the project with the authority in charge of roads. The farmers committed themselves to build these roads with their own tools and labour. The roads benefited many families and solved many problems related to the transportation of products and inputs.

— The home improvement program, which channeled surplus income toward the improvement of the standard of living. Also the training given through courses and demonstrations on nutrition, health, housing improvement, clothing and home food production, and the success reached by the pre-school program.

— The productivity of the main production lines, which increased significantly as a consequence of the generation of technological packages adjusted to the conditions of the region.

ON INSTITUTIONS

The Cáqueza project was seriously limited by two basic constraints: first, the existing institutional structure was inadequate to encourage the adoption of new technologies, and second, the organizations of the region worked without any coordination due to institutional jealousy and rivalry between the officers.

This caused some frustration among the members of the project team, who were trying to obtain a higher adoption rate of the new technology. In an effort to fill the gap between the existing institutions and their clients, the idea arose for what were later called "buffer institutions."[15]

The following institutions deserve to be mentioned: the ICA-Caja Agraria credit program, the Committees for Development, the Marketing Cooperatives, the Corn Production Plan, the Marketing Plan, the Onion Production Plan, and the Pre-school Program. Some of these succeeded, others failed, but their importance rests on their having perceived the need to coordinate the action of the institutions working on rural development. Later this led not only to a national strategy for rural development, but to institutional changes in harmony with it, since both technological and socioeconomic changes are closely linked to the institutional changes necessary to achieve the planned objectives.

ON THE ICA

The development approach set in motion by the Cáqueza project produced a considerable change in the Colombian view of rural development, particularly within ICA. It was acknowledged that although ICA had adequate resources to do agronomic research, it lacked the knowledge and experience to pass their results on to the small farmer. The new development concept arose mainly as a result of the great amount of new information generated on the relationship between the technical and socio-economic problems linked to rural change.

METHODOLOGICAL RESEARCH FOR RURAL DEVELOPMENT

In the past ICA's approach to research was concentrated mainly on commercial agriculture and large farms. It was assumed that the research results were independent of the size of the farms and that therefore those results would be suitable for small farmers as well as those with large holdings[4]. The first experiences in Cáqueza demonstrated that this idea was not completely valid and that a good part of the technology generated by ICA was inadequate for small farmers. The research strategy that emerged in Cáqueza encouraged the other rural development projects in the country to adjust their recommendations to the characteristics of each region.

The original emphasis on high-production technology has been superseded by a new effort to offer an improved technology that is in accord with the limitations confronting the small farmer.

Besides this new orientation in production, the first marketing crisis in the project area (a direct consequence of the emphasis on production) made technicians aware of the need to start considering non-biological factors as well. As an answer to the problem of institutional risk (mainly changes in the sale price of products) the project designed a marketing plan to form a vertical coordination system for the marketing of perishable products, consumption products and agricultural inputs[14].

The fact that, at the end of the fifth year of the project's operation, ICA had set up a technical support group to help the other projects to adjust their recommendations to local production conditions, indicates that the concept of on-farm research had gained acknowledgement.

Another meaningful impact of the Cáqueza experience on ICA's structure was the creation in 1977 of the Research Program for Multiple Cropping to generate the necessary technology for this common cultural practice among small farmers.

In the long run, these methodologies will certainly produce important effects on Colombian traditional agriculture, because they have recently been adopted at the national level.

FACTORS THAT RESTRICT THE ADOPTION OF TECHNOLOGY

As a consequence of the strategy set in motion by the project, it was possible to identify some of the main constraints to the adoption of technology by small farmers.

One of the main constraints was risk[2]. At the beginning, the project assumed that the low yield of some crops, particularly corn, was due to lack of technical knowledge on the part of the farmers. After two years of experimental work it was realized that the low adoption rate was due to inadequacies of the technology. In a study that compared traditional technology with recommended technology it was found that the latter required three times the expenditure for inputs and most of these expenses had to be paid in cash. Although the recommended technology could triple the yield and double the profits, the risk increased 15 times.

Most of the suggested technological innovations (especially seeds, fertilizers and pesticides) had to be purchased and therefore the small farmer was forced to ask for credit. In other words, he had to obtain loans in order to become an innovator.

When the project realized that the farmers objected to the use of credit, it was decided to study this matter thoroughly, and thus it became possible to clarify the problems related to the costs of credit: complicated and excessive procedures and the risk associated with debts[10].

As a solution, the project developed an experimental credit program with shared risks that was intended to reduce the cash requirements for farmers so that they could use the recommended technology. The strategy originally known as the Production Plan for Small Farmers, is now called the Risk-Sharing Plan for the Adoption of Technology[13].

The plan was started in 1974 with 27 farmers growing 11.6 hectares of corn in two municipalities. During the first experience, the lowest yield was between 1000 and 1500 kg/ha among 22 percent of the farmers. They all surpassed the area's traditional level of 800 kg/ha. The following year the project extended the plan to onions, obtaining better results than with corn, since onions are a commercial crop that generates considerable profits.

At present the strategy is being tried outside the Cáqueza Project in four ICA regions, 21 municipalities and 10 agricultural and one cattle species, in an area of 271 hectares involving 502 farmers. It is hoped that this will help to perfect the strategies and will provide a basis for change in the present system of institutional credit.

TRAINING IN RURAL DEVELOPMENT

The diagnostic study carried out by the project in its first stage, besides providing a number of variables, became also a real "spiderweb of problems" for technicians to investigate. The need for studies and the limited capability of the scarce human resources available led to a new strategy that was very well accepted, especially by centres of higher education. This strategy was designed to set up the project's "research requirements," and consisted of a series of small and well-defined studies linked to one another[11], in which students from a number of universities, especially the post-graduate program of the National University and ICA, participated. These small studies made it possible to compile most of the basic information on the limitations and requirements confronted by small farmers.

During the five years of the project, 129 publications, including research studies, evaluations and reports, were produced[15]. These publications helped to increase the knowledge of those responsible for the research as well as those who read them.

The project also increased the formal training of its personnel at all levels. With the IDRC's support, ICA took two very important steps to increase the capability of its personnel. The first was the support provided for graduate studies on rural development, the second the setting up of the National Training Program in Rural Development (PNCDR).

In 1975 there were only five professionals specializing in rural development. By 1978 there were 32, mainly agronomists and veterinarians. In general, the activities can be summarized as follows: three studies at the PhD level, 40 MSc dissertations, four PhD theses and 11 Bachelor's theses. In the Cáqueza Project, three agronomists and one sociologist were trained at the Masters level, three agricultural and cattle-raising experts and one veterinarian attended short courses[15].

The PNCDR offered short courses and service training for all the personnel of the country's projects at the Cáqueza Training Centre (built with the IDRC's support) and at the Rionegro Training Centre (also adapted as a training centre with IDRC funding), located in two different areas of the country. This program gave important teaching participation to Cáqueza personnel. The training of field personnel working in rural development was accomplished through short courses, with the basic purpose of promoting understanding of development, traditional agriculture, its problems and the experience acquired.

Up to 1978, a total of 51 courses had been given at the two training centres, with 1,213 participants — agronomists, veterinarians, home economists, agricultural and cattle-raising experts, and family educators. The majority of personnel trained were middle-level technicians.

The results of training were very positive, particularly in the following respects: it improved the knowledge and techniques of field personnel, enabling them to understand the limitations of the small farmer and to transmit information to him; at the graduate level it strengthened the knowledge of ICA personnel in fields unrelated to biology (particularly communications) and it contributed to the orientation of research.

IMPLICATIONS FOR INSTITUTIONS AND DEVELOPMENT POLICIES

The work carried out by the PDRs (including Cáqueza) was developed during a period in which agricultural planning was being attempted from the base up (base programming) and not the other way around, as had been the case during the rural extension period[8]. However, the actions of the PDRs were organized over the existing institutional structure of the area. The establishment of new institutions to respond to the needs of the farmers was not foreseen, because it was expected that the PDRs would point out those needs and would promote the organization of participation groups and the development of programs through the most suitable institution.

The constant flow of information from the field as a result of base programming made it possible to detect:

a) The lack of coordination within the institution responsible for the generation and transfer of technology: researchers had no knowledge of the limitations and needs of the extension agent's clients who, in turn, had no knowledge of the latest technical progress made by researchers and the way in which they could participate in the activities of rural development.

b) The lack of dialogue between ICA and other service institutions such as those related to credit, marketing, infrastructure and social welfare.

Through this flow of information, the lack of coherence between the objectives of these institutions and the real problems of the small producer became evident. Some examples may illustrate this:

In credit: Loans were granted in amounts less than the real production costs, and in the case of multiple cropping, to finance just one crop.

In marketing: Many actions were undertaken but none aimed at solving the problem of the wide and constant fluctuations in the price of products.

In social welfare: Food of high nutritive value went to population groups with low nutritional standards, without providing them with suitable information on its use.

In infrastructure: Public works were undertaken following political criteria rather than the felt needs of the community or the priorities of the region.

Technical assistance: Technical recommendations were transferred that had neither been tested nor adjusted to the region's specific conditions. The most important lesson derived from these experiences, not only in Cáqueza but in other PDRs as well, was that there is often a great difference between what the farmer really wants and what institutions and planners consider to be his needs.

An important step was taken during the preparation of loans for the present Program of Integrated Rural Development (DRI). The experts provided by the donor agency dedicated considerable time to the personnel and documents of the Cáqueza Project, which were later to influence the orientation of the agricultural and cattle-raising planning of the National Planning Department (DNP) and some institutional reforms.

One way or another, the positive and negative experiences of the project have made a significant contribution to the establishment of rural development methodologies. For example, the research approach at the level of productive unit and priority production systems (called "technological adjustment") are part of the present development strategy of the Technological Transfer Districts. The Marketing Plan, in spite of its unpretentious results and the small impact it might have had on the community, seems to have played an important role in showing the DNP the importance of market limitations and the type of approach required to overcome them.

COMMENTS

The following are some unexpected factors that arose during the implementation of the development model in the Cáqueza Project. These factors should be kept in mind in planning future programs.

a) Any such program requires simple and concrete work methodologies that allow for their own gradual improvement.

b) The program officers should understand the importance of information, so that they methodically compile and use it for their own benefit. This will make possible a true evaluation of the impact made by the project, as long as there are no obstacles or requests for political reports, which usually tend to distort reality.

c) There is a need for planning that makes it possible to visualize priorities and assign the necessary resources in time to permit the projects uninterrupted development. For example: the need to make a market analysis before starting to transfer technology, otherwise there will be marketing problems for the product, as it was the case in one instance; the need for efficient training of project personnel in their various activities before executing the programs. It is the project's experience that it takes considerable time for technicians of any level to become knowledgeable about the field in question, and the philosophy, objectives and methodologies involved.

d) The government institutions present in the area and involved in the design of the program must also orient their programs anew. The most important change to be made is the efficient assignment of roles so as to eliminate duplication or obstruction.

REFERENCES

1. Brown, L. and E.P. Eckholm. Crisis mundial de alimentos? The Overseas Development Council. Washington, 1974. 13 p.

2. Cobos, A. Retribuciones económicas y adopción de tecnología en maíz con crédito ordinario y crédito compartiendo riesgo. Tesis M.S. UN-ICA, Bogotá, 1976. 134 p.

3. Escobar, G. y K.G. Swanberg. El nivel de vida como componente de la estrategia de desarrollo rural. Instituto Colombiano Agropecuario. Bogotá, 1972. 18 p. (mimeo).

4. Gonzalez, R. y H. G. Zandstra. El pequeño agricultor: Filosofía de la investigación en producción agrícola del pequeño agricultor. ICA-CIID, Bogotá, 1975. Tomo 1. 36 p. (mimeo).

5. Instituto Colombiano Agropecuario. Agricultura tradicional y moderna en Colombia: consideraciones sobre el dualismo tecnológico (capítulo 3). Instituto Colombiano Agropecuario, Bogotá. (no date). 165 p. (mimeo).

6. _____ . Experiencias en desarrollo rural ICA-CIID. Instituto Colombiano Agropecuario. 2 ed. Bogotá, 1975. 102 p. (mimeo).

7. _____ . Justificación de la estrategia y un modelo para el desarrollo rural. Instituto Colombiano Agropecuario, Bogotá, 1972. 21 p. (photocopy).

8. _____ . Política de desarrollo rural. Instituto Colombiano Agropecuario, Bogotá, 1975. 46 p. (mimeo).

9. Jaramillo, H. y R. Ojeda. Consideraciones generales para una definición de estrategias en desarrollo rural. Instituto Colombiano Agropecuario, Bogotá, 1974. 25 p. (mimeo).

10. Morss, R.E., J.K. Hatch, D.R. Mickelwait and C.F. Sweet. Strategies for small farmers development: an empirical study of rural development projects. Development Alternatives Inc., Washington, 1975. V. 1. 497 p.

11. Nestel, B., K.G. Swanberg and C.A. Zulberti. The Cáqueza Project. International Development Research Center, Bogotá, 1976. 23 p.

12. Zandstra, H.G. Experiences of rural development projects as related to the study of comparative agricultural systems. Presented at the CIAT Agricultural Systems Planning Sessions, Cali, 1973. 8 p. (typed).

13. _____ y C.A. Villamizar. Plan de inversión en producción para pequeños agricultores. Instituto Colombiano Agropecuario, Bogotá, 1974. 17 p. (mimeo).

14. _____ , K.G. Swanberg y C.A. Zulberti. Venciendo las limitaciones a la producción del pequeño agricultor. IDRC — 058 s, Bogotá, 1975. 32 p.

15. _____ , K.G. Swanberg, C.A. Zulberti y B. Nestel. Cáqueza: Experiencias en desarrollo rural. Centro Internacional de Investigaciones para el Desarrollo, Bogotá, 1979. 386 p. (being printed).

CHAPTER TWELVE

ADVICE ON THE FACTORY FLOOR

PRABHAS CHAKKAPHAK

Small-scale industries in Asia often need basic advice to improve their products or processes, but cannot afford to pay for it. Extension services are available in many countries, but they vary in effectiveness and their services are not always known to industries, especially those in neighboring countries. In 1972 the IDRC approved a grant of $1,180,000 to be spent over five years to support existing national industrial extension services. The grant was also designed to strengthen the capacity of the technical information services of the National Research Council of Canada to respond to queries from developing countries. Further grants of $162,000 and $1,675,000 have since been approved.

 PRABHAS CHAKKAPHAK is director-general of the department of industrial promotion, ministry of industry, Bangkok, Thailand. An economist, he received his education at several U.S. universities, with additional training at the Federal Reserves Bank of New York, the customs and treasury departments in Washington, the World Bank and the National Defense College. Dr Prabhas has served in Thai government posts since 1947.

THE FIRST CONCERN of developing countries is to establish industries and provide funds from financing sources. But as industries flourish, many problems will surface that are traceable to technical and technological aspects.

The problems of many small-scale industries in Asia cannot be solved by "book" solutions — solutions often inspired by experiences and successes in more developed economies. Present industries are often ineffective because of excessive costs, particularly through wastage or improper use of raw materials, or because their products are of low quality resulting from poor methods of production. To overcome these problems, industry needs technological advice.

Quite often, the advice needed is very basic — it is not a question of providing advanced technology, but of having an experienced engineer or technician look at a plant and make suggestions that will improve the processes or the products. Unfortunately, many of these small industries cannot afford to pay for such services in their earlier stages of development.

Industrial extension services in Asia vary according to the level of development of each country and the types of organizations set up to provide these services. But all clearly recognize the need to provide technological advice on equipment, methods and processes, production techniques and quality control. And they are determined to obtain the personnel and resources to provide this advice to production managers on the factory floor.

Because of the wide differences between countries in language, cultural background, types of industry and levels of industrial development, the industrial extension services must be staffed by indigenous engineers or technicians. They must also complement services in management, marketing and financing, which are equally important. Extension services thus should be organized nationally, or perhaps even by province and city.

No service organized for a region as a whole could be expected to provide satisfactory service to individual factories. But a regional service could provide resources on which national extension services could draw; a regional service could also provide a focus that would facilitate cooperation and exchanges between national extension services and help link them into a functional network.

THE TECHNOLOGY GAP

There can be no doubt that all types of assistance programs are important and should be provided for the development and growth of small industries. Evidence indicates that most of these programs are successful and have contributed to the industrial progress of developing countries in Asia. However, much has yet to be done to provide the appropriate technology that will enable small industries to survive the competition from large modern enterprises and those from overseas. Understandably, technology is often neglected because of inherent difficulties in providing this type of assistance and the lack of technically-trained manpower in the public sector.

A technological gap exists not only between urban and rural industries, but also between large and small ones. There is an even greater technological gap between industries in developed nations and those in developing countries. To overcome these problems, small industries need technological information and a "delivery system" that will effectively bridge this gap. This delivery system will, to a large extent, have to rely on people who can provide technological advice right on the factory floor.

Industrial extension worker visits a furniture factory in the Philippines.

No one denies that the industrialized countries and the international agencies could be more effective in stimulating the diffusion of technology. But there is a growing realization that the greater part of man's technological know-how is already freely available. The problem is that the developing countries are ill-equipped to find, evaluate and apply it. By strengthening the capabilities of its participating organizations, TECHNONET aims to facilitate the transfer of technology and its assimilation to small-scale industries.

Developing countries have much to share with each other, and the developed countries, through their technical assistance programs, can strengthen this capability. In fact, TECHNONET draws upon the technological resources of various cooperating organizations in developed countries for some of its activities. For example, the National Research Council of Canada's Technical Information Service (NRC/TIS), with its thirty years of experience in serving Canadian industry and its international reputation, backs up TECHNONET's technical information needs when it has access to material pertinent to Asia. Similar arrangements have been made with other centres of technical information.

THE TECHNONET APPROACH

TECHNONET Asia is a voluntary cooperative network of organizations in nine countries of the region, engaged in the development of industry, particularly smaller scale industry, through the transfer of technical information and the provision of extension services.

The project is a voluntary "cooperative" one in the sense that, while IDRC provides money, material and equipment, the participating national organizations, all concerned with small industry development, agree to certain responsibilities. For example, they agree to make available to one another readily obtainable industrial technical information on products and processes in their countries; to receive personnel from other participating organizations for observation, training or discussion; to make available technical personnel for short-term assignments to other participating organizations; to arrange visits of industrialists from participating organizations to local industries, organizations and institutions.

The organizations involved also develop coordination and liaison amongst themselves with local institutions concerned with the development of small and medium scale industry, and local sources of technical information.

The countries and organizations involved in TECHNONET are: Bangladesh (Bangladesh Small and Cottage Industries Corporation), Hong Kong (The Hong Kong Productivity Centre), Indonesia (Department of Industry), Korea (Korea Scientific and Technological Information Center), Malaysia (Standards and Industrial Research Institute of Malaysia and the

Council of Trust for Indigenous People), Philippines (Institute for Small-Scale Industries, University of the Philippines, and the Economic Development Foundation), Singapore (Singapore Institute of Standards and Industrial Research), Sri Lanka (Industrial Development Board of Sri Lanka), and Thailand (Department of Industrial Promotion, Ministry of Industry).

TECHNONET Centre, currently located in Singapore and headed by an administrator, is the focal point of the network. It provides continuous liaison and coordinating services and support for the activities of the participating organizations.

The heads of the participating organizations, together with the administrator, comprise a Council which meets at least once a year and concerns itself with policy aspects. Two technical committees created by the Council — one on information and one on training — also meet regularly. An executive steering committee, composed of Council members, was formed recently to chart the future structure and framework of TECHNONET.

The Centre is fully supported by IDRC, with a funding allocation for a total of seven years — phase one for $3\,1/2$ years (1973-1976) and phase two for another $3\,1/2$ years (1977-1980). The combined total spent on TECHNONET operational activities by IDRC and the participating organizations is approximately US$1 million annually. This is considered a relatively modest amount in comparison with what would be necessary to undertake similar activities without the benefit of a network.

HIGHLIGHTS OF THE PROJECT

In phase one, 1973 to 1976, the TECHNONET Project produced results that are attracting considerable attention. The most important are:

A strong network of organizations that share the common goal of developing industrial extension and information services for small- and medium-sized industries. They make available to one another industrial technical information on readily obtainable products and processes in their own countries. Empirical evidence indicates that technical information obtained from countries at similar stages of development is far more useful and relevant than that imported from highly developed countries. Participating organizations also make technical personnel available to each other for short-term assignments. Visits of personnel from participating countries to local industries and institutions are also arranged. A bi-monthly TECHNONET Digest keeps participating organizations informed on the latest technological developments in countries within the network.

The nucleus of a group — some 1,200 practitioners — who see industrial extension as a valid professional activity. More than 15,000 extension cases involving factory visits are currently being handled each year. In addition, approximately 10,000 technical enquiries are being handled each year by correspondence, telephone or personal contact. Formal training programs, seminars, and workshops have been undertaken for industrial extension and information officers to upgrade the capabilities of participating organizations.

Observation, training, and discussion visits — as appropriate — have been arranged within the network. In 1975, the Asian Industrial Extension Officers (ASINDEX) Forum, under the aegis of TECHNONET was created to give added impetus to this emerging profession. The bi-monthly TECHNONET Newsletter facilitates communication between extension and information officers. It also publishes industrial extension case histories handled by participating organizations, which could be of value to others.

Governments now increasingly accept the need for this type of service and allocate resources for its further development. As a result, since 1973 industrial extension and information services for small and medium industries have been given high priority in government development programs. Activities now range from computerized technical information services — available in two participating organizations with the possibility of two others eventually being computerized — to industrial extension services on a provincial level in many of the participating organizations. In the process, networks on a national level have also been encouraged and developed.

While all the participating organizations have terms of reference that permit them to be active across the entire industrial sector, experience has shown that needs are greater in some types of industry than in others. To identify priority industries, a list of industries has been agreed upon, in order of their degree of need for technical information: (1) Metals, (2) Food processing, (3) Wood-based industries, (4) Plastics, (5) Packaging, (6) Electrical appliances and products, (7) Agricultural waste utilization, (8) Ceramics, (9) Rubber products, (10) Footwear, (11) Leather, (12) Construction building materials.

State-of-the-art reviews have been undertaken to pinpoint problem areas and the assistance needs of specific industry groups. These broad industry classifications are now being further refined in order to arrive at more specific areas of activity. A matrix of expertise, sources of information in participating countries, and centres of excellence in specific fields has been encouraged to minimize the wasteful duplication of efforts. For example, the establishment of a Plastics Technology Information Unit within the Hong Kong Productivity Centre and the upgrading of the Foundry Workshop at the Industrial Development Board of Sri Lanka have been supported, with the understanding that their expertise and facilities will be available to all other participating organizations. IDRC has also partly supported the establishment of the Asian Packaging Information Centre and the International Ferrocement Information Center. The Institute of Small-Scale Industries of the University of Singapore has made available to participating countries its modern low-cost automation laboratories as well as its excellent training facilities.

The Singapore Institute of Standards and Industrial Research has made available to all participating organizations its excellent Current Awareness Service. Other participating organizations are now in the process of setting up centres for specific industry areas — not necessarily with the financial support of TECHNONET — whose programs will be tied into TECHNONET's long-range activities.

The following are a few examples of industrial problems successfully handled by extension officers trained by TECHNONET-sponsored training courses.

MECHANICAL KNIVES FOR CUTTING BAMBOO

The Malaysian Handicraft Board had a problem increasing the rate of splitting bamboo trunks, an essential raw material for local handicraft. A Malaysian, who was trained at INDEXTRAC I, designed a mechanical knife with eight cutting blades. With this, the rate of production increased to at least four times what it had been before.

The same extension officer designed a knife for use with the same machine to cut the split pieces of bamboo into thin strips, as used in many hand-crafted items. The traditional method was to whittle each piece of bamboo to strips by hand with an ordinary knife. This was time-consuming and uneconomical because of a high rate of wasted material. With this knife, production rose steeply and was further matched with a dramatic increase in yield from raw material.

GLUE MIXER

A glue manufacturer wished to increase his production. Previously he had the appropriate mixture stirred in a drum by hand, which was cumbersome and ineffective. An INDEXTRAC-trained extension officer contributed to the design and fabrication of a simple mechanical mixer, at very low cost, which has now been put to use satisfactorily.

NUTS AND BOLTS

During an industrial visit, an INDEXTRAC trained extension officer came upon a small company that could not market its production — nuts and bolts — because of sub-standard quality. He and his colleagues found a way to provide the firm with the necessary information concerning the required quality standard. They also helped to determine the correct raw materials and treatment to achieve the desired results. The manufacturer is now able to market his products and is looking to SIRIM's extension officers for further assistance in selection and purchase of machine tools to further expand his business.

WOOD-CRAFT

A Filipino manufacturer of wood products such as trays and mugs faced two main problems. First, a high percentage of finished products warped and cracked. Second, a high percentage of raw materials had to be rejected because the firm could not get rid of wood colour defects that appeared after staining.

With the help of extension officers trained at INDEXTRAC II, the warping and cracking were determined to have been caused by improper seasoning and drying. Subsequently, the firm was given detailed drawings of a new kiln combustion chamber and sketches with which to modify and improve the drying chamber. Finally, the correct type of staining medium for acacia sapwood was identified, correcting the colour defects. All these helped alleviate the manufacturer's problems.

GOLD WIRE

A Singapore manufacturer of gold wire for use in integrated circuits had a problem of low yield caused by breakage. The wires were made of 99.9 percent pure gold, drawn to a diameter of 0.001 inch through a series of diamond dies using a soap-based lubricant.

Through TECHNONET Centre's Technical Enquiries Service, with NRC/TIS backing, the problems were determined to have been caused by work-hardening, impurities in the gold, and the soap-based lubricants used in the process. Information regarding proper stress-relieving methods and necessary filtration of the lubricant was furnished the manufacturer. This has helped in significantly reducing the losses caused by breakage.

ELECTROPLATING

Thai extension officers trained at INDEXTRAC II were asked to help solve an electroplating firm's problem — cracking and pitting of nickel-plated products. The extension officers visited the plant and discovered that the electroplating solution used was both off specification for pH and also contaminated. Starting with fresh solution and setting rigorous "standard procedures" to control strength and purity, and establishing maintenance and cleanliness standards throughout the process area not only solved the problem but also improved sales. Several similar enterprises have since been assisted following this first successful extension activity.

CAST IRON PIPE FOUNDRY

A Malaysian foundry made cast-iron moulds for spun pipes by drilling a four-inch bore in solid cast iron rods one foot in diameter and ten feet long, using a heavy duty lathe and boring head. This resulted in heavy toolwear and eccentric bores.

With TECHNONET Centre's help, SIRIM's extension officers investigated and concluded that a "sand-core" rather than a "solid-core" casting technique would solve the problem. Since this had already been tried unsuccessfully by the foundry, the extension officers examined the results in detail and were able to determine that the sand-core composition was wrong. By adding necessary ingredients such as pelleted pitch and wood flour, and applying compressed gas, the "sand-core" casting technique was successfully demonstrated and subsequently adopted by the foundry.

LINGERIE

Owners of a Filipino lingerie factory wished to increase production efficiency which persistently remained at only half the rated capacity of the plant. When extension officers first visited the factory, a disorderly work flow was particularly noticeable. Tracing the flow by section and by machine to determine the appropriate flow-rate from one processing stage to the other, a more functional layout for the plant was drawn up. At the extension officers' recommendation, two supplementary machines to relieve the most serious bottlenecks were installed, and within a week production efficiency increased to a satisfactory level.

Based on this success, the firm has since relied upon the extension officers to help them further with management problems, including cost and quality control, book-keeping, production planning and even personnel administration.

CAR PARTS

Two extension officers during INDEXTRAC III's fieldwork session were assigned to investigate the possibility of increasing the productivity of a small firm's manufacturing section. Through careful and methodical in-plant observations and interviews, the priority need was determined to be machine and method improvement, which could be expected to result in immediate and significant productivity increase.

Production bottlenecks in several operations were then identified and appropriate corrective measures recommended. They were accompanied by several practical engineering design sketches for modification of the most essential machines, and also descriptive details necessary for production method improvement. The recommendations — with expected improvements in cost, productivity and even product quality — were so convincing to the owner/manager that he implemented all measures promptly and has never looked back.

FOUNDRY WORKS

An extension officer in Sri Lanka revisited a foundry after having attended INDEXTRAC III. His previous extension visits had resulted in his determining that the factory needed a centre lathe and a bench drill. However, his latest visit, after the training, enabled him to help the non-ferrous foundry in many more ways. He noticed particularly that the furnace and burner, the most critical equipment to this type of industry, were both primitive and inefficient. Fuel combustion was incomplete and there was no temperature control. Production method and quality control were also problems that contributed to high production costs.

The officer prepared sketches for a new furnace with a high-efficiency burner. Strict procedures were also laid down to minimize deposits of impurities on castings. The factory manager is extremely pleased with the results, and especially with the great improvement to the extension service that has become available to him because of INDEXTRAC's training.

THE IMPLICATIONS

The experiment is by no means completed. The approaches and specific activities undertaken continue to be critically evaluated and improved upon. But already some lessons may be learned from the results that could be of immense value to international and national agencies involved in development assistance and funding.

By effectively deploying a proportion of its own technological manpower for advisory work, a developing country can be technologically much more self-reliant than has hitherto been imagined.

What is most needed is not fancy new systems, but an indigenous capacity to apply well-known and readily available technology to overcome actual problems as they are encountered on the floors of the factories there today.

The transfer of technological information can be effectively achieved if properly processed — in this case by the industrial extension officer. This officer acts as the link between the entrepreneur, who often is not capable of recognizing his problems and identifying his needs, and the sources of information, which can provide more relevant information when requests are more specific.

Developing countries have much to share with each other in terms of technological information, processes and expertise. What is needed is the stimulus to spur on this co-operation and interchange — and at times bring this capability to the surface.

The so-called transfer of technology is not a one-way affair, from developed to developing countries. In some cases, as shown by actual experience, developing countries have the capability to make this transfer a two-way affair.

Much of the experience gained from the experiment has previously been theorized. What is revealing, however, is the fact that TECHNONET Asia is in the process of demonstrating that such concepts as "self-reliance" and "cooperation" are not mere slogans. They can be made to work. The investment of IDRC in the project is worth imitating throughout the developing world.

Much more has to be done in making technology accessible to small industries. The technological problems of small industries in the developing countries of Asia are vast and varied. In countries represented in TECHNONET Asia alone, we are catering to an estimated 450,000 small industries. And we are possibly reaching only a small number of these establishments. It is clear that many agencies have a role to perform if we are to achieve the objectives we envision: industry and professional associations, technological R&D institutes, the educational system, and other public and private institutions devoted to technology. More important, the cooperation and active involvement of government policymakers and legislators is necessary.

One of the major objectives of TECHNONET — always implicit in phase one, and now particularly stressed in phase two — is the development of a self-reliant activity that will be able to continue into the future when IDRC funding tapers off or ceases. This objective has the strong endorsement of the participating organizations, which have taken the necessary steps in this direction. At the Council meeting in September 1978, it was unanimously resolved that TECHNONET Asia should continue and that it be transformed into a legal organization. The details are now being finalized by an executive steering committee formed by Council.

APPROACH TO SELF-APPRAISAL

In the past five years of the TECHNONET Asia Project, a considerable volume of experience has accumulated through its "regional voluntary and cooperative network" approach to small industry development. The approach has had its share of "mid-course corrections", resulting not only from various shortcomings but also from substantial accomplishments. Most important is the lesson that might be learned from the TECHNONET experience by other organizations that may carry out similar undertakings in other parts of the world, and there are indications that this may soon happen. To complete this exercise, however, requires more than simply an "external" evaluation. Notwithstanding TECHNONET Centre's ability to make an impartial appraisal, all of TECHNONET's participating organizations need also to review, critically and objectively, the changes — beneficial or otherwise — that have resulted from their involvement in the project. Some of the critical questions that need to be answered through self-appraisal include:

— what national and/or institutional goals have been established, or are being established that are directly attributable to the existence of the network?

— what tangible effects have resulted from the direct networking efforts between and among the participating organizations?

— what changes have taken place in strategy and operational methods of the various participating organizations as a result of exchanges of views, experiences and other interactions within the network?

To be truly worthwhile, a substantial portion of the answers to such questions needs to be sought from the practicing industrial extension personnel of the participating organizations. It is they who are on the "extension front". Practically speaking, they are in the best position to clearly perceive the changes that may have taken place as a result of TECHNONET's involvement. Not only do they experience the effects on the participating organization's side, but also that of their clients. This feedback from the grassroot level if properly acquired and managed, would surely help the organizations to understand the needs of the country's small industry sector, measure how such needs are being met, and determine to what extent the accomplishment may be attributable to TECHNONET. Only through such a deliberate process can a learning pattern be properly set out for the benefit of networks-to-be in other parts of the world.

CHAPTER THIRTEEN

MAKING INFORMATION ACCESSIBLE

FERNANDO MONGE

Information about what is going on in their field is essential to researchers. It is particularly important for those working on cassava because until recently little research was being done on the crop, despite the fact that it is a food staple for 200 to 300 million people. This chapter describes a new approach to providing information to cassava workers and the creation of a Cassava Information Centre, one of a worldwide network of centres providing highly specialized information to agricultural researchers. The project was funded initially with an IDRC grant of $57,500 in 1972 and $218,750 in 1976.

FERNANDO MONGE is an Ecuadorian who currently is coordinator of the Scientific Information Exchange Unit at the Centro Internacional de Agricultura Tropical in Cali, Colombia. As such, he is responsible for the project he describes in this chapter. Dr Monge holds degrees in agriculture, plant genetics and mass communication, and has done post-doctoral work in information sciences. He was recently elected president of the Inter-American Association of Agricultural Librarians and Documentalists.

T HE CENTRO INTERNACIONAL DE AGRICULTURA TROPICAL, CIAT, was created on the basis of experience acquired previously at the International Rice Research Institute (IRRI) and the Centro Internacional de Mejoramiento de Maiz y Trigo (CIMMYT). The success of these centres is due mainly to their clear orientation of contributing to the solution of food-production deficits in the world, using a commodity-oriented strategy rather than the more traditional academic, discipline-oriented research approach.

Although information has always been recognized as a major support component of research activities at the international centres, the traditional "library approach" was followed, without taking into account recent developments in information science. During 1972, while CIAT was still in its formative years, the Cassava Production Systems Program was expanded to a level of major importance within CIAT's research activities. This was the result of a significant contribution from the International Development Research Centre which considered the crop a potential solution to the calorie deficit existing in a considerable segment of the world's population.

IDRC recognized the importance of having an information service that would actively interact with research activities from the initiation of the program. Initially, the plan was to collect all existing information on cassava at CIAT and then compile a traditional bibliography based on citations only. After further analysis of the Latin American situation, further conversations were held with IDRC information scientists, and it was decided that this was not the most beneficial course of action. In this chapter, we present the major considerations that led to the creation of the Cassava Information Center at CIAT and the establishment of a system of *consolidated information* that provides a wide range of services far beyond the traditional library approach.

Because of the success of this information centre, others such as the International Grain Legume Information Centre at IITA and the Sorghum and Millets Information Centre at ICRISAT were established within the international agriculture research centres (IARCs). The International Irrigation Information Centre in Israel, although not directly related to the IARCs, is another example of a successful centre following the same general principles and also established through IDRC's financial assistance.

POPULATION AND FOOD PRODUCTION

Elaborating on the world's long-run capacity to produce food, the Committee on Resources and Man of the U.S. National Academy of Sciences calculated that food production could reach a level nine times the present production. This increase would be possible by quadrupling production from the land and increasing production from the sea two-and-a-half times. This assumes reaching maximum productivity from all potentially productive land, and also presupposes a greater use of fertilizers, insecticides and fungicides, and the chemical or microbiological synthesis of foods as well as other innovations[11].

On the other hand, population increases have implications that go beyond the mere balance between birth and mortality rates. Frejka[5] points out that a significant part of the population increase has to be accepted as an accomplished fact. The present ratio of 30:70 between the rich and poor countries' populations, for instance, will inevitably become 20:80 and perhaps 10:90 in years to come. In addition, FAO statistics already indicate a marked increase of the dependent population in Latin America, where over 40 percent of the population is under 15 years of age and thus does not represent a production factor.

In conclusion: "The population of this globe is now doubling every 35 years and currently increasing at an estimated rate of 75 million people per year. This means that there will be over 200,000 more people for breakfast tomorrow morning than there were today; and that, in order to just stay at present levels of nutrition, man will have to learn in the next 35 years how to produce as much *more* food per year as he has since dawn of history. Production will need to be doubled in the next 18 years to meet the anticipated combination of increased population and purchasing power"[9].

INFORMATION: ESSENTIAL FOR RESEARCH

Institutionalized research focusing on problem-solving activities appears as a potential solution for increasing food production in the world. Information, on the other hand, is an essential factor within the research process, not only in terms of accomplishing a coordinated action to avoid duplication of efforts but also to obtain a multiplier effect sometimes called "a cross-fertilization of ideas".

Several communication and development models postulate three sub-processes to which distinct and sometimes institutionalized groups of people correspond. These are the generation of knowledge, its transformation and transmission, and finally, its application and utilization. In the agricultural sector, for instance, knowledge is typically generated by scientists, usually in government or private research institutions; transformation and dissemination is accomplished by "change agents" who belong to extension institutions or communication services; and finally, farmers represent the users who apply this knowledge.

This same structural model can be used to visualize the more restricted system of scientific development. The one *sui generis* characteristic of this subsystem, however, is that the same group of people — scientists — assumes the various roles of knowledge-generators, transmitters and users.

But where does information fit into this broad, structural scheme? Contrary to what happens in development models, information does not have a box in this scheme because of its dynamic nature and the connecting role it plays. Instead we prefer to conceptualize information not as an end in itself, but as an indispensable means that, through the process of communication, *interconnects the elements of the scientific research system to make it work as a system* and not as a heap of unconnected and disorganized parts.

Consequently, it is surprising so frequently to see information and communication services that are totally divorced from the research process. If researchers have sometimes been criticized for creating "ivory towers", perhaps librarians and documentalists are also guilty of creating "paper towers" because of a failure to recognize this *cycle of knowledge* as one single process.

Immediately a question comes to mind: are Latin American scientists unproductive only in terms of publishing research results or also in terms of *producing* results? In other words, are they not publishing because they do not have any research results to publish? In this connection, Felstehausen[4] points out: "Each year the Latin American countries produce hundreds of reports, papers and articles on agriculture and rural development. Despite this fact, many of these publications and reports are not available to the administrator, planner, professor or scientist for whom they were written. The majority of agricultural materials are produced and distributed in limited numbers. Few agricultural reports in Latin America are collected and preserved systematically."

Based on the scant evidence we have, it seems that: 1. The low publication rates observed in Latin America are due mainly to a lack of motivation (institutional incentives as well as personal interest); 2. The rates are not due to a concommitantly low rate of production of research results; and 3. The majority of research results are not published in standard communication channels but in so-called unconventional forms, such as mimeo-graphed papers and pamphlets, in limited numbers, and even in letters and memoranda. A minor percentage of this information reaches annual reports and proceedings of conferences and symposia.

Certainly, very valuable research results are produced, but they remain in the laboratories, the scientists' offices, or their secretaries' files. Diffusion is minimal.

THE LATIN AMERICAN SCIENTIST AS INFORMATION PRODUCER

Very little research has been done in Latin America on this aspect. It is recognized, however, that production of technical and scientific literature is low. A first study carried out by Rheineck and Diaz-Bordenave[12] analyzed 34 scientists at La Molina University in Lima, Peru, in terms of certain institutional and personal variables that could have a bearing on their litera-ture production. The results indicated that motivation seemed to play an important role in their publication rates. Personal motivation was low and, in turn, appeared to be based on a lack of perceived institutional incentives to publish. Over 50 percent of the scientists sampled were not aware of the existence of any reward whatsoever for the effort of publishing an article.

In a follow-up study carried out by Diaz-Bordenave[2] on a more international sample of 88 scientists attending a meeting of the Latin Ameri-can Association of Agricultural Scientists (ALCA), similar results were ob-tained. Based on this information, the author notes: "Priority reasons for this phenomenon seem to be centered around the motivational field, both from the standpoint of the scientist himself (interest) as well as the institution (in-centives)." And after presenting results where 66 out of the 88 scientists in-cluded in the sample stated that "publishing is not necessary" or that "pub-lishing makes a contribution but it is not really necessary," the author con-cludes: "It is evident that in Latin America no 'publish or perish' (ethic) exists."

THE PUBLICATION INFRASTRUCTURE

In 1962 the Scientific Development Division of the Pan-American Union and the Scientific and Technical Documentation Center of Mexico, through a National Science Foundation grant, supported a study of Latin American journals of science and technology. Despite the time lapse, the re-sults of this study still reflect the present situation: "Typically, scientific and technical journals published in Latin America are short of personnel. Selec-tion and edition of articles, as well as other editorial functions are usually carried out by scientists and professors in their free time, frequently free of charge. Budgets are usually small and printing and distribution costs are subject to unpredictable raises due to inflation. Runs are small and the reduced number of subscribers limit the income that would come from subscriptions and advertisements . . . It was found that around one-third of the journals did not have a regular frequency of appearance, and if they did, it was seldom met in practice . . . It was also found that most journals had a low periodicity, quarterly at best, they were frequently irregular and of a reduced size (three out of every ten journals had less than 50 pages per issue)"[10].

Ten years later, Gorbitz[6] confirmed these results at a meeting of a group of technical editors in Puerto Rico. In addition, he noted the uneven quality of the contents, a high percentage of journals having a short life cycle and poor international distribution.

Nevertheless, in spite of all these problems, it is rather comforting to see in Lawani's list[7], later published in a more complete form by Brennen[1], of the 50 most frequently cited journals in the tropical and subtropical literature, that 6 Latin American titles are included.

It is not difficult to infer from the fundamental lack of motivation to publish observed in a major portion of the scientific community, that most Latin American technical and scientific journals are weak and constantly menaced. The infrastructure of technical and scientific publication in Latin America is another illustration of the vicious circle of underdevelopment. This, however, is a challenge to Latin American documentalists to develop innovative systems adapted to the real situation in order to reach the appropriate audiences with pertinent information at the time it is needed.

THE LATIN AMERICAN SCIENTIST AS INFORMATION CONSUMER

The other side of this production/consumption equation is also low. Latin American scientists exhibit a low level of information-seeking behaviour, but we do not have to go into elaborate psychological explanations in order to explain this phenomenon.

In a previous study[8] it was found that the relative ease of access to pertinent information was the most important variable for explaining the use made of libraries by a group of Colombian scientists. This result has been confirmed by the success of the Cassava Information Center at CIAT and has thus become a guiding principle in our program. Latin American scientists are eager to receive information in their fields of research, but the generally poor services offered constitute a barrier that soon produces a sense of futility.

Whereas in the more developed countries such as the United States, one dollar of every five spent for goods, services, construction and new machinery is allocated to information services, in Latin America library collections are usually poor and out-dated, the number of libraries is very small, they are usually located only in major cities, and the services offered are of the traditional type. This is what we call the "cafeteria approach" to information management, where the librarian or documentalist's function becomes one of displaying materials for users to choose.

The net result of this complex of factors is, therefore, as follows. Given that only a very low percentage of the information produced in the less-developed countries ever reaches conventional publication channels, and that only a very low percentage of the information generated in the more developed countries ever reaches the libraries and documentation centres of the less-developed countries, we can conclude that Latin American scientists are minimally informed in their respective fields.

Consequently, the tasks facing the scientist's counterpart, the documentalist, are first to collect the so-called "fugitive" material produced in the less-developed countries i.e., internal reports, mimeographed papers, etc., which contain valuable and up-to-date information. Second, he must link the vast amount of information produced and collected in the developed countries with users in the LDCs, in such a way that users are not bogged down with nonpertinent information. And, thirdly, he must process, group and disseminate information in a manner that reaches the user directly at the appropriate time.

CIAT'S ANSWER: CONSOLIDATED INFORMATION

Undoubtedly, the key variable for success in an information system is easy access to information by the users. Thus the fundamental principle of CIAT's Scientific Information Exchange Unit is to take the information to the user and not to wait for the user to request it. The scientist's time should be reserved, as much as possible, for the activities in which he is a specialist. Conversely, the information specialist should be allowed to fulfill his own role, which is to understand the needs of his client thoroughly and provide him with all pertinent materials.

In order to accomplish this, however, services feasible within the limitations of an underdeveloped environment must be developed. A prerequisite, of course, is a good collection of books and journals and a minimum of equipment such as copiers and storage and retrieval equipment.

The Scientific Information Exchange Unit at CIAT, a major part of which is the Cassava Information Center, has at present a library with approximately 40,000 volumes and receives 1302 journals regularly. The library does, of course, operate as a regular specialized library, but more important, it provides certain personalized services.

CONTENT PAGES

This is a current awareness monthly publication that lists the tables of contents of selected journals. Three areas are covered: animal sciences, covering 350 journals; plant sciences, covering 300 journals; and social sciences, covering 58 journals. They are distributed to almost 2000 scientists in Latin America, who select articles of their interest and request photocopies.

Although initially this service was directly distributed to individual subscribers, the unit is now stimulating national institutions to act as distributing agencies for their countries. At present, nine countries have adopted this system with highly rewarding results; for instance, the School of Agronomy Library at the University of Buenos Aires has almost doubled its output of photocopies from the time the CIAT *Content Pages* were first distributed among Argentinian agricultural scientists as a service of the country's national information system.

As a result of this service, CIAT provided around 250,000 pages of technical literature in photocopy form to Latin American scientists in 1978.

DOCUMENTATION

ABSTRACTING SERVICE

The documentation process considers typical scientific articles (published in journals or as manuals, research bulletins, internal reports, mimeographed papers, etc.) as the unit of information in order to make an in-depth analysis and produce an abstract and keywords or subject-matter descriptors, which are later used for selective retrieval of the information. The final products are cards containing this information, which are then distributed 10 times per year to over 2000 scientists in the world. On the basis of these abstract cards, scientists may request photocopies of the complete articles.

Documentation services cover four areas: cassava, in which the Center has the only known complete collection of everything published on this crop; field beans, limited to literature applicable to tropical environments; tropical pastures and forages; and Latin American agricultural economics and development.

Although documentalists working in these areas are professionals in their respective fields, the service counts on the invaluable collaboration of the scientists in the various research programs at CIAT. This symbiosis produces a beneficial effect both for the scientists, who are supported by a rapid and complete literature service, and the documentalists, who can count on a consulting body of specialists in order to perform an accurate analysis of the information.

The most complete collection of information on cassava in the world.

SPECIFIC TOPIC SEARCHES

Information retrieval is accomplished through a mechanized system based on specific topic descriptors. Searches are performed in an average of 15 to 20 minutes, which makes it usually possible to answer queries the same day they are received. This service is widely used by scientists around the world. Requests received by cable from subscribers are answered immediately, also by cable, giving the numbers of the pertinent documents since subscribers have the entire collection of abstract cards. In this manner, our collection of documents is being used for retrospective searches by users in distant countries with practically the same speed as if they were at CIAT headquarters.

CUMULATIVE VOLUMES

At the end of the year, the Center classifies all abstract cards produced during that period into broad categories and publishes cumulative abstract volumes, which are distributed to subscribers and sold to non-subscribers. To date, four volumes have been published on cassava, three on beans, three on Latin American agricultural economics, and one on tropical pastures and forages. Cassava and bean abstracts are published simultaneously in English and Spanish while the other two areas are published only in Spanish.

SERVICE FEES

The Unit charges nominal fees for all services provided, since free services tend to be under-valued. To facilitate payment, a system of coupons was created; a special agreement for payments to be effected in local currencies has also been reached with the Inter-American Institute of Agricultural Sciences (IICA), which has country representations in all Latin American capital cities.

CONSOLIDATED INFORMATION

An efficient documentation service must have several essential characteristics. It must: reach the user directly; provide a surrogate of the document (an abstract or annotation); incorporate a selective dissemination of information capacity in order to perform specific topic searches according to individual interests; and it must provide a photocopying service for document delivery.

Nevertheless, the concept of consolidated information goes beyond typical documentation activities. It includes not only the collection and dissemination of the products of research, but also mechanisms that synthesize these into scientific and technical knowledge that contributes to the advancement of science and can be applied to the solution of pressing problems.

Consequently, the process of consolidating information includes an evaluative phase whereby an expert in a broad area of knowledge selects and analyzes for reliability and quality the existing information at a given time, and then condenses and fuses this information in other types of publications such as monographs, state-of-the-art reports, and practical application manuals.

In accordance with this concept, the Cassava Information Center at CIAT produces:

1. *Monographs* on specific areas which are based on all the pertinent literature as provided by the Center's abstracting service, and give the user the benefit of a critical analysis of the subject by world experts.

2. *Field manuals* on practical problems, which gather, for example, information on diseases, pests, nutritional deficiencies, etc. and translate it into simplified language accompanied by colour illustrations. These manuals are thus useful not only to the researcher but also to the farmer and to the extension agent.

3. *Reproductions of published articles* which, because of their importance, deserve a wider distribution than they would get through the journals themselves, especially considering the limited access that most Latin American libraries and scientists have to technical journals. Frequently these reproductions are translations into Spanish.

4. *Newsletters* such as the *Cassava Newsletter*, which try to answer the question: Who is doing what and where? These publications have primarily a journalistic function of making scientists aware of research in progress and other news in the field and promoting cohesion through communication among researchers.

TRAINING

The First Agricultural Documentation Course presented by the Center was attended by 16 participants from 11 Latin American countries. The main purpose of this two-month course was to instill in the participants a philosophy of rapid, efficient service and to prepare them to work under restricted budgets with techniques appropriate to the LDCs. In addition to the operating functions, administrative aspects were also dealt with.

ACCOMPLISHMENTS AND FUTURE TRENDS

The basic accomplishment of the Cassava Information Center at CIAT may be the introduction of a pragmatic approach to the handling of technical information in the Third World. Emphasis is placed on satisfying the scientists' needs rather than on the techniques of doing so, which at times may be more complicated than necessary. The Consolidated Information model for collecting and disseminating information on a commodity-specialization basis and producing services that reach the users promptly is being adopted at both the national and international level. It has attracted the interest of larger international systems such as AGRIS (FAO) and AGRINTER (IICA), and it may be considered a pilot model for coordinated information services for other agricultural commodities in the LDCs.

Because of the wide acceptance that these services have had, present activities are being directed increasingly towards training of personnel for national documentation services, networking the documentation activities of the IARCs and other national and international organizations, and to increasing the coverage of literature within the four selected areas.

The present demand for training in documentation may be partially a result of CIAT's training activities in general, since all CIAT trainees are exposed to these services during their training period. Moreover, they receive free a one-year subscription in their area of interest after they return to their countries. In this manner, an awareness of the importance of efficient information services in research has been created at the national level, resulting in the desire for similar services at their own institutions.

The excellent results obtained with the first course have reinforced the decision to offer this type of training on a regular basis, together with follow-up activities such as meetings with former trainees at CIAT, so as to provide opportunities for exchanging experiences and to promote a feeling of a Latin American working team of colleagues.

As far as networking is concerned, the IARC's are in a privileged position in which to establish a worldwide efficient information system on priority food commodities. As a result of a meeting of the IARC librarians at CIAT four years ago, IITA (Nigeria) began a food legume documentation centre, focussing initially on cowpeas, under the auspices of IDRC. In 1978 the Cassava Information Center provided advisory services to the Sorghum and Millets Documentation Centre at ICRISAT (India), another IDRC-sponsored activity.

Given the tremendous information explosion, we feel that the present trend to this type of highly specialized information centre is the most viable solution, and offers the best possibilities of reaching users rapidly.

IDRC has played an innovative role in foreign aid programs for the LDCs. Rather than being dogmatic, IDRC policy has always been flexible and open-minded, permitting the incorporation of firsthand experiences into programs and services. The results of this attitude are programs such as the Cassava Information Center, which have met with success without upsetting the socioeconomic milieu.

LITERATURE CITED

1. Brennen, Patrick W. Documentation in the Literature of Tropical and Subtropical Agriculture. Special Libraries. 65(7):263-271, July 1974.

2. Diaz Bordenave, Juan. Resultados de una encuesta realizada en la VII Reunión Latinoamericana de Fitotecnia. Secretaría de la ALALF, Octubre 1968. 16p.

3. FAO, Estado Mundial de la Agricultura y la Alimentación 1976. FAO, Roma, 1976.

4. Felstehausen, Herman. Improving Access to Latin American Agricultural Information through Modern Documentation Centers. University of Wisconsin Land Tenure Center, Mimeo No. 68LTC-1, Bogotá, Colombia, January 1968. 15p.

5. Frejka, Tomas. The Prospects for a Stationary World Population. Scientific American. 228(3); 15-23. 1973.

6. Gorbitz, Adalberto. Evaluación de Revistas Científicas Latinoamericanas. Fitotecnia Latinoamericana (Venezuela). 8(2):23-29. 1972.

7. Lawani, Stephen. Periodical Literature of Tropical and Subtropical Agriculture. UNESCO Bulletin for Libraries 26(1):88-93.

8. Monge, Fernando. Reading habits of scientists in a Colombian Institution. University of Wisconsin, Madison, Wis., Ph.D. Thesis, 1967, 213p.

9. Nickel, John. Dicurso Inaugural. Centro Internacional de Agricultura Tropical, CIAT. Noviembre 19, 1974. 12p.

10. Pan American Union. Latin America Scientific and Technical Journal Publication: A Statistical Analysis. In: Pan American Union, Guide to Latin American Scientific and Technical Periodicals. Washington, D.C. 1962. pp. 161-187.

11. Paz, Luis J. Trabajo presentado en la Mesa Redonda sobre la Producción y Demanda de Alimentos en América Latina y el Caribe. 13a. Reunión Anual de la Junta Directiva del Instituto Interamericano de Ciencias Agrícolas de la OEA. Caracas, Venezuela, Mayo 14-18, 1974.

12. Rheineck, Fritz y Diaz Bordenave, Juan. Factores Asociados con la Producción de Literatura Científica por Investigadores Agrícolas. Instituto Interamericano de Ciencias Agrícolas de la OEA, IICA, Dirección Regional para la Zona Andina. Mimeo. 17p., Agosto 1967.

PART THREE

AN ASSESSMENT

CHAPTER FOURTEEN

THE ROLE OF RESEARCH IN SOLVING PROBLEMS OF THE DEVELOPING COUNTRIES: A THIRD WORLD VIEW

VINYU VICHIT-VADAKAN

This chapter examines the role of research in developing countries in the solution of their problems, the difficulties faced by researchers and the potential users of their products, the role of external financing agencies, and, lastly, the author's own experience with IDRC's funding policies.

 DR VINYU is director of the United Nations Asian and Pacific Development Institute in Bangkok, Thailand. Himself a Thai, he is former dean of the faculty of economics at Thammasat University. Educated in economics and international studies in Switzerland, he was a fellow of the World Bank's Economic Development Institute in Washington in 1967. Dr Vinyu's particular research interests lie in development planning and the problems of urbanization.

A T THE RISK OF OVERSIMPLIFICATION, some general observations may be made of the present state of the art in research in the developing countries. It is widely recognized and accepted by all concerned that although policy- and action-oriented research is mutually beneficial to both the researchers and users of their products, there is still a lot of room for improvement in this area. In actual practice, research is neither recognized nor accepted as a high priority by policymakers. Indications of this include the budgetary allocations for research at the governmental level and the lackadaisical interest of potential users of research products.

There is a serious lack of understanding and even communication between research generators and research users. This is reflected in many forms, including mutual suspicion and distrust. There is also a general under-utilization of research capacity in most developing countries. Such existing excess capacity could be usefully tapped.

Although there is very close contact in many instances between researchers in developing countries and researchers in the western world, there is a very serious gap in contacts between researchers in the Third World countries themselves. The existing North-South contacts stem at least partly from the fact that many of the researchers in developing countries were — and are still being — educated in the west, and their links with their institutions have been scrupulously kept.

WHAT HAS GONE WRONG WITH RESEARCHERS?

The attitude of potential users of research products in developing countries, though not always defensible, does indicate that there are quite a few things wrong with the community of researchers, who are mostly located in the academic (or para-academic) institutions in the countries.

Research products are too abstract: ivory tower research is not very useful to policymakers and practitioners. There is a lack of interest and sometimes a positive aversion on the part of researchers to undertake research and studies that are policy- or action-oriented, and there are always long delays in coming up with research results. At any rate such results are not often produced in time to make them available and usable to policymakers and practitioners.

The researchers themselves, in many instances, consider their task completed when they have written up their findings. There is a serious lack of interest among researchers in following up on their work by either disseminating their findings to a larger audience or assiduously trying to sell their findings to potential users.

WHY ARE RESEARCH PRODUCTS NOT USED?

From the standpoint of the researchers, it is generally felt that the government agencies, which constitute the majority of potential users of policy- and action-oriented researches, always unrealistically look for immediate results and immediate solutions. These unrealistic demands on the part of the users cannot be satisified by the research community.

Most governments have a very short-term outlook and perspective and are not interested in long-term trends and implications of their policies, an area in which the researchers can probably contribute most. Governments are usually too preoccupied with day-to-day crisis management, for which the contribution from academic researchers is little or none.

Policymakers and practitioners do not grasp, and are not convinced of, the importance of concepts and theories; and the output produced by the academic research community is always looked upon as irrelevant and full of incomprehensible jargon.

PROBLEMS FACED BY RESEARCHERS

Apart from the negative view that potential users in the public sector hold about research products, the researchers themselves encounter a lot of other difficulties in their work.

The western type of education that most researchers have lays a good deal of emphasis on specialization in a narrowly-defined area. This does not lend itself to policy- and action-oriented research, which needs to be done in a wider context and on an interdisciplinary basis. Nor are the tools and facilities the researchers would have used during their education, such as model-building and computerization, readily available in developing countries. This is further complicated by the difficulty of either obtaining the types of data required or ensuring their reliability in adequate detail for meaningful research.

There is always the question of political sensitivity in any policy-oriented research which is, in many instances, difficult for researchers to handle. In pursuit of their future careers, researchers also have to make the difficult choice between having their research products published in internationally-recognized and prestigious academic journals, for which the treatment of the subject matter should be theoretical and quantitative, and undertaking an action-oriented study that may be directly relevant to potential users but academically not very rewarding.

Consideration has to be given to revising the allocation of the researchers' time between research and training which in many instances is prescribed by the institutions with which the researchers are affiliated. Quite often, emphasis is placed on teaching, where there is an immediate need and, therefore, a higher priority in the academic institutions. This situation is made more or less permanent by a chronic shortage of teachers. The cumbersome administrative rules and regulations imposed by funding sources, whether domestic or external, also result in researchers spending a lot of time on research administration rather than on its substantive aspects.

An interdisciplinary team of researchers needed for policy- and action-oriented research is very difficult to put together and manage. And priority areas for policy- and action-oriented research activity are equally difficult to define because in most instances the policy of the governments in this regard is not clearly defined.

Another common problem for researchers is lack of access to government data, which may be due to the confidentiality of such information. In other instances, re-packaging of raw data collected by various government agencies is not as easy as it seems to be. In such cases, researchers have to rely on readily available data that are usually incorrect or insufficient or both, and they therefore have to resort to collecting primary data themselves. Thus their research projects often end up being much more expensive and time-consuming than originally expected.

SOME OBSERVATIONS AND FUTURE OUTLOOK

In spite of all the difficulties and constraints, the situation in the developing countries is not all that bad, and the future can be looked forward to quite optimistically for a number of reasons.

Even in the past, research products were being used by agencies, governmental or otherwise. Research in the hard sciences, technological research in such areas as agricultural techniques, industrial improvements and biological studies, always had a ready clientele who would make use of the research products as they were produced. This was less true of the social sciences and humanities. But there is an observable trend that shows they are being made use of more than in the past.

The fact that some of the key problems are identified and recognized is a very important step forward. The problems identified and recognized include those listed earlier, such as the communication gap between researchers and potential users. It can certainly be expected that solutions to these problems will be found very soon. In fact, in some developing countries, very important progress has already been made in this direction. It is just a matter of time before such problems will be largely solved in most of the Third World countries.

A well-developed institutional framework is now established to promote the South-South contacts in all the regions. These regional networks or groupings serve the common purpose of promoting contacts, dialogues and interactions among researchers and research institutions in the developing countries. They are all gaining strength and popularity among the participants.

There is also a large amount of observable and tangible feedback in the form of real and beneficial use of research products as reflected in the curricula of training programs of academic institutions in developing countries. Training curricula at universities now have many more subjects on local situations and local problems. This has a direct effect on the availability of training materials dealing specifically with the issues and problems of the developing countries. Moreover, academic institutions in developing countries nowadays offer more of an interdisciplinary treatment of subjects and issue-oriented programs.

These trends are quite encouraging, and one can optimistically look into the future role of research in solving the problems of the developing countries.

THE IMPACT OF FOREIGN FUNDING AGENCIES

Research funding in the developing world varies in its pattern from one country to another. It would not be correct to draw a sweeping conclusion on this issue. But again some general observations may be made.

RESEARCH FUNDING SOURCES

There are a number of sources to which researchers and research institutions address themselves for funding. Domestic sources include the regular budget allocations of the research institutions themselves, the government allocations on research support to universities and institutions, and sources that researchers or their institutions can identify elsewhere in the country, including foundations and even the private sector. Intergovernmental bodies, such as agencies within the United Nations family and other international organizations, constitute another valuable source of funds. The developed countries also make contributions to research funding for the developing countries, through government-to-government arrangements, research institutions in the developing countries, or directly to the researchers themselves. And finally there are the semi-governmental, non-governmental agencies, foundations and private sector sources. Such bodies, mainly in the developed countries, constitute an important element in the provision of research funds to developing countries.

The magnitude of these various categories of sources varies from one country to another, and from one institution to another. There are also variations over time.

CRITICISMS OF FOREIGN FUNDING SOURCES

The positive impact of foreign funding sources will be dealt with later. At this stage, it may be advisable to look into some of the criticisms.

The first and probably the most important criticism that scholars in developing countries have made of external research donors concerns the role they play in research undertakings vis-a-vis that of the researchers themselves. Though it is true that there are as wide variations among donors as among the recipients of research funds in regard to circumstances surrounding their relationships, a general observation is that funding sources exercise their own preferences and priorities. It is common to find research funding agencies that have their own pre-determined priority areas and programs and that their research funds are made available mostly to researchers interested in undertaking studies in such areas. Unfortunately in these cases the researchers and scholars in developing countries are reduced to being mere data collectors to provide empirical evidence for points of view the donor agencies would like to propagate. There have even been instances where the local counterparts do not have access to the research product.

A number of research funding agencies still would like their own or their country's interest to be served by the end-product of the research, and make this an important criterion for research grants. There are several examples of research funds made available to scholars in developing countries only if the proposal indicates the involvement of the donor country's institutions, and only if the research deals with some aspect of the recipient country's relationship with the donor country. Sometimes it is even stipulated that a part of the research take place in the donor country.

Many donors are output-oriented and limit themselves to financing "low risk" research through known and established researchers in developing countries. This practice has resulted in overloading the established researchers and not providing sufficient opportunity for young scholars to make known their talents. This unfortunate practice is especially true in the social sciences.

Donors also place undue emphasis on the international comparability of research outputs, and much less attention to the usefulness of the research products in the countries. There is a feeling among scholars and researchers that, although both components should be there, the emphasis might be the other way around.

In only very few instances do external donors contribute adequately to institution building. Most of the available research funds are for specific projects, and once completed, there is very little left behind for the recipient institution to follow up.

Finally there is the simple fact that research funds are not easy to come by. It is much easier to get external assistance in large amounts for development projects, consultancy services and training programs. Research activities are always looked upon, and in some cases justifiably so, as high-risk ventures with uncertain output and intangible results.

POSITIVE IMPACT

In spite of all the criticisms made of external funding sources for research in developing countries, there is obviously also a considerable positive impact, and this aspect should not be lost sight of.

Although variations naturally exist among countries, institutions and programs, external funding sources play a vital role in research undertakings in developing countries. These external sources are a very useful supplement to the research community in most, if not all the developing countries of the world.

External sources have an important catalytic effect in generating local counterpart research funds. The mere requirement for a counterpart contribution, either in cash or in kind, in many instances makes the difference between whether such a project would be launched or not. External sources also usually provide the needed seed money for institution building. Foreign funding agencies play a vital role, too, in setting up and strengthening regional bodies and networks which otherwise would not exist there at all because of the lack of resources and low priority given to such institutions by national governments.

Priority areas, as defined by external donors, sometimes assist local researchers in broadening their perspectives and later enable them to look at local problems more fruitfully. External donors also play a most important role in the promotion of collaboration in research among developing countries. Without them, there is little chance for researchers to learn about the work of their counterparts in other developing countries. This aspect has a useful long-term effect, in that once contacts are established the researchers will keep in touch long after completion of the research projects.

IDRC FUNDING POLICIES

The news of the establishment of the IDRC and its policies in early 1970 was most welcome. It came to me personally as a pleasant surprise. During the previous two decades, in various capacities, I had the good fortune of being both a producer and a user of research. I had the benefit of having associated myself with and having been involved in a number of research activities and institutions, and was, therefore, in touch with a variety of donors. My extensive travel also brought me in touch with various intellectual communities in many parts of the world. My feelings and sometimes misgivings about research in developing countries and the role of foreign donors are already reflected in the earlier sections of this chapter.

The long-awaited and welcome policies of the IDRC include:

— the fact that research priorities would be largely determined by people in the developing countries themselves;

— even high-risk projects would be considered by the Centre, particularly those proposals emanating from lesser-known, younger researchers among the Third World academic community;

— there would be an element of institution building or strengthening of local capacities for research in the developing countries;

— the Centre would be willing to support the promotion and enforcement of South-South collaboration in research so that there would be more contacts and joint programs among the researchers in developing countries; and,

— there would be minimal emphasis on research administration, and minimal application of rules and regulations on IDRC-funded undertakings.

Having been among the first recipients of IDRC research assistance in 1972 and having had a continued association with IDRC-assisted activities since, I can claim to be in a good position to pass judgment on the Centre's policies. I can state unreservedly that at least until now the Centre has lived up to the expectations of many in the intellectual communities of the Third World.

To illustrate the point it may be useful to cite some examples of IDRC-assisted projects and programs in which I have been personally involved. Four examples are given as illustrations: the choice of these four was made because of the different aspects of the IDRC aid-relationship they reflect.

STUDY ON THE URBANIZATION OF BANGKOK

This is a part of four country studies in Indonesia, Nepal, the Philippines and Thailand. The Bangkok study tried to look at the history of the city and determine how it had survived and become a city of five million people, 40 times larger than the next largest city — without a plan, without land-use control, and without a sewerage system. The content, data and methodologies were the choice of the team of researchers. Apart from being among the first projects funded by IDRC, it was the first time in the country that an interdisciplinary and inter-institutional team of researchers was formulated. Unknown junior researchers also formed part of the research team. It certainly was a high-risk project and proved to be so because the completion date was delayed by almost two years. But lessons were learned in the process, particularly relating to the interdisciplinary, inter-institutional aspects and the involvement of junior researchers. Since then a large number of research undertakings in the country have followed this approach: it was IDRC's risk-taking that changed the research environment in the various academic institutions in this country.

CAMS

The Council for Asian Manpower Studies is a grouping of Southeast Asian scholars interested in the general area of economics and demography. The executive committee, composed of Asian scholars, decides on the priority areas for research, farms out research activities to national institutions, provides research funds to them and administers and manages the research projects. The IDRC is a member of a consortium of five donors who provided funds to CAMS which in turn decides on the projects, researchers and all other relevant details. CAMS has been in operation for almost a decade now, and apart from having completed a number of research projects, it has built up research management capabilities in its own secretariat for research undertakings on an international scale.

ADIPA

The Association of Development Research and Training Institutes for Asia and the Pacific was started in 1973 with a membership of less than 30 institutions, and has grown to include more than 130. The vital role played by the IDRC was institution building: it provided funds for the secretariat, the publication program and the project development meetings. These meetings merit further elaboration. At the biennial general meeting of the Association, the membership decides on priority areas for collaborative research and training programs. The secretariat, with financial assistance from IDRC, organizes project development meetings of institutions interested in each of the program areas. This enables the interested member institutions to get together with their counterparts in other countries to work out possible collaborative research programs. During the last few years 13 such groups were formed; all of them, with no exception, came up with collaborative programs that at the moment involve some 65 member institutions, or half the total membership. It should also be noted here that the association does not provide any research funding for these collaborative undertakings. Each participating institution has to arrange for its own research funds. Out of 13 programs going on at the moment, only one collaborative research was funded by the IDRC. This simply illustrates the fact that the IDRC's investment in such undertakings has a very high multiplier effect, as it had in this case, and has provided the opportunity for scholars in developing countries to get together with their counterparts in other countries — an opportunity that otherwise would not have existed.

DEVELOPMENT INFORMATION PROGRAM

This is a program jointly organized by the UN Asian and Pacific Development Institute and the National Institute for Development Administration of Thailand. It was conceived as part of the global undertaking of the IDRC on development information (DEVSIS). The IDRC is among the major donors of this program. It is a regional activity for Asia and the Pacific, trying to look at the role of information in the total process of development planning for developing countries. Studies were commissioned and meetings were conducted with assistance from the IDRC. The Centre's role here has been catalytic. It came in with its assistance at a very early stage of the program where the risk element was indeed high. It is now gratifying to note that other donors have joined in and the program is expanding rapidly.

The previous four examples were presented to illustrate how useful and crucial the role of the IDRC has become. Without its timely assistance, none of these programs would be as active or as productive as they are now. The fact that IDRC was willing to gamble with an institution in a developing country on something that may be very innovative in nature, untried and without any assurance of positive results, has made its contributions much appreciated by the recipients. It is not easy to find other donors playing this kind of risk-taking role. With the successful experience of the IDRC, more donors now are willing to gamble with high-risk projects.

FINAL THOUGHTS

I sincerely believe that the IDRC has started well. I would also like to express my earnest hope:

— that the IDRC will keep on moving in the same general direction of filling the gaps that exist at the moment;

— that expanding financial power does not corrupt its well-established reputation;

— that the expanding size of the Centre does not turn it into another monolithic bureaucracy; and,

— that other financing institutions can learn from the experience of the IDRC and follow its pattern.

We in the developing world need more IDRCs.

APPENDIX I

EXCERPT FROM
THE INTERNATIONAL DEVELOPMENT
RESEARCH CENTRE ACT

O BJECTS AND POWERS OF THE CENTRE

4. (1)   The objects of the Centre are to initiate, encourage, support and conduct research into the problems of the developing regions of the world and into the means for applying and adapting scientific, technical and other knowledge to the economic and social advancement of those regions, and, in carrying out those objects

a) to enlist the talents of natural and social scientists and technologists of Canada and other countries;

b) to assist the developing regions to build up the research capabilities, the innovative skills and the institutions required to solve their problems;

c) to encourage generally the coordination of international development research; and

d) to foster cooperation in research on development problems between the developed and developing regions for their mutual benefit.

(2)   The Centre, in furtherance of its objects, may exercise any or all of the following powers in Canada or elsewhere, namely the power to

a) establish, maintain and operate information and data centres and facilities for research and other activities relevant to its objects;

b) initiate and carry out research and technical development, including the establishment and operation of any pilot plant or project, to the point where the appropriate results of such research and development can be applied;

c) support or assist research by governments, by international, public or private organizations and agencies, or by individuals;

d) enter into contracts or agreements with governments, with international, public or private organizations and agencies, or with individuals;

e) give recognition, by such means as the Centre deems appropriate, for outstanding contributions to international development by international, public or private organizations and agencies, or by individuals, and publish and otherwise disseminate scientific, technical or other information;

f) sponsor or support conferences, seminars and other meetings;

g) acquire and hold real property, money or any interest therein and alienate the same at pleasure;

h) acquire any property, money or securities by gift, bequest or otherwise, and hold, expend, invest, administer or dispose of any such property, money or securities subject to the terms, if any, upon which such property, money or securities is given, bequeathed or otherwise made available to the Centre;

i) expend, for the purposes of this Act, any money appropriated by Parliament for the work of the Centre or received by the Centre through the conduct of its operations; and

j) do such other things as are conducive to the carrying out of its objects and the exercise of the powers of the Centre.